Written by

R. M. DAVIS
JEWEL DILLON
KAREN MYERS
MARYALICE PASLAY
DAN RIGDON
JAMES STEWART

This book is designed for personal or group study.

PENTECOSTAL PUBLISHING HOUSE
8855 DUNN ROAD
HAZELWOOD, MO 63042-2299

# Word Aflame Elective Series

Spiritual Growth and Maturity

WHY? A Study of Christian Standards
Bible Doctrines—Foundation of the Church
Salvation—Key to Eternal Life
The Bible—Its Origin and Use
Strategy for Life for Singles and Young Adults
Spiritual Leadership/Successful Soulwinning
Your New Life
Purpose at Sunset
Values That Last
Meet the United Pentecostal Church International
Facing the Issues
The Holy Spirit
Life's Choices
Alive in the Spirit
A Look at Pentecostal Worship
A Look at Stewardship
Financial Planning for Successful Living

## Family Life Selections

The Christian Youth
The Christian Woman
The Christian Man
The Christian Parent

## EDITORIAL STAFF

R. M. Davis ................................. Editor
P. D. Buford ..................... Associate Editor

J. L. Hall ......................... Editor in Chief
United Pentecostal Church International

©1984 by the Pentecostal Publishing House, Hazelwood, Missouri. All rights reserved.
Reprint History: 1984, 1985, 1987, 1989, 1990, 1992, 1994, 1998, 2000, 2004
ISBN 1-56722-060-6

CURRICULUM COMMITTEE: James E. Boatman, P. D. Buford, Daniel L. Butler, R. M. Davis, Gary D. Erickson, Jack C. Garrison, J. L. Hall, G. W. Hassebrock, Garth E. Hatheway, Vernon D. McGarvey, David L. Reynolds, Charles A. Rutter, R. L. Wyser.

# Foreword

**C. M. BECTON**
**Harvestime® Speaker**
**United Pentecostal Church International**

So often it is felt that when you are filled with the Holy Ghost, it is the ending rather than the beginning. One wonders how this concept ever came about as we certainly do not have that feeling about a natural newborn baby. Ask any parent if they feel this way. If that baby does not grow and develop, the parents' hearts are filled with great anxieties. This is similar to the newborn Christian who, like a baby has many things to learn and, in fact, is beginning a lifetime of learning.

This series helps put spiritual growth and maturity into proper perspective. It starts out with having the right attitude, which is all important, and proceeds to all the ingredients that will help make you a well-balanced Christian. It not only covers positive traits but also deals with the other side.

Christians are often criticized for being unrealistic. However, Christians tend to focus more attention on the positive side of life than the negative, the hope of tomorrow instead of situations of today.

The old "tough it out" philosophy of the pioneer days is rarely found in our world of shallow roots and conditional commitments. God's people march to a different drummer. The underlying tone of Scripture is one of growth and endurance, not escape.

These lessons offer a muscular message that includes some sweat and tears. The process of growing and maturing is not easy. We are never promised a dreamy, fragrant rose garden, but we are given a strong exhortation to walk a consistent path of discipline. Our faith needs fiber in order for us to do battle against passive attitudes. A stand must be taken if we hope to finish the course victoriously.

Are you a soldier of the Cross, a follower of the Lamb? Do you hope to be carried to the skies on flowery beds of ease? All Christians must face foes, mountains, valleys and should live a consistent life in this world that is no friend to a child of God.

We are not different because we are free of problems, but because we have a power with us that the world cannot claim. This power enables us to face any and all things that come our way.

You will find realism and encouragement in each of these studies based on scriptural principles. These principles provide the diligent Christian with spiritual direction and truth that never fails.

# Contents

| Chapter | Page |
|---|---|

Foreword ............................. 3

1. Attitude Is the Key .................7
2. Loyalty—The Way of a Godly Life ....19
3. Teach Us to Pray ..................31
4. The Spectrum of God's Love ........43
5. Survival Kit for the Depressed ......55
6. Gifts that Edify ...................68
7. The Ministry—God's Gift to the Church .......................... 80
8. The Bible—Our Sure Foundation .... 92
9. Praise and Worship ...............104
10. Spiritual Healing for the Church ....115
11. The Ministering Church ...........127
12. Redeeming the Time ..............138
13. My Place in My World ............150

# Attitude Is the Key

*Therefore all things whatsoever ye would that men should do to you, do ye even so to them: for this is the law and the prophets.*

*Matthew 7:12*

---

### Start With the Scriptures

Matthew 5; 6; 7; 10:38;
  18:6, 21-35; 25:31-46
Romans 12:3

I Corinthians 13:1-7
Ephesians 4:21-32
Philippians 3:7-14

---

Mark Hazen greeted his co-workers with his usual infectious smile and cheerful "good morning." During the mid-morning break, he laughed and joked with his colleagues as usual. In his dealings with others throughout the day, he was pleasant and supportive.

In fact, a casual observer would think that Mark was having a good day. He would not know that Mark's wife was scheduled for surgery the next week, that a two-day business trip Mark had been looking forward to was canceled, that his daughter was in bed with the flu, and that he was just recovering from it himself. In addition, the observer would not detect that Mark's chronic back problem was bothering him. In spite of his multiple problems, Mark maintained a positive attitude.

Across the hall, Alan Jensen arrived thirty minutes late. With a scowl on his face, he barely nodded to his secretary before entering his office and closing the door.

His secretary braced herself for the criticism she knew would be forthcoming during the day. She felt sorry for anyone who might need to talk with Alan.

What was Alan's problem? His car had failed to start, and he had to call his motor club to send someone to assist him.

These two men reacted very differently to life's difficulties. In any given situation, when one person sees difficulty as a stumbling block impeding progress, another sees it as a challenge—a stepping stone to new learning experiences and greater success. Attitude is the key.

A person with the proper attitude looks on the bright side of things. He can find something positive even in negative situations. He is a joy to be around. His presence can lift the spirit of one who is downhearted, cheer one who is sad, and comfort the bereaved. In trying times, he is a source of strength.

How does one keep a positive attitude even in distressing circumstances? The answer is found in the greatest Book of all: "Thou shalt love the Lord thy God with all thy heart, and with all thy soul, and with all thy mind, and with all thy strength: this is the first commandment. And the second is like, namely this, Thou shalt love thy neighbour as thyself. There is none other commandment greater than these" (Mark 12:30-31).

This directive indicates three areas of relationships

where a positive attitude is important: one's attitude toward God, one's attitude toward others, and one's attitude toward himself. These areas are so interrelated that a problem in one area will affect the others. If one's attitude toward God is not what it should be, this fact will be apparent in attitudes toward others and toward himself. By the same token, if a person does not have the proper attitude toward himself, his attitude toward God and toward others will be strained.

Although they are entertwined, let us look at each of these three areas separately.

## Attitude Toward God

In one's human frailty, he is unable to love God with all his heart, soul, mind, and strength. To do so, he must have God's Spirit of love within.

*Salvation.* When a person comes to God in repentance, is baptized in Jesus' name for the remission of sins, and receives the infilling of the Holy Ghost, he is filled with love. The Holy Ghost is God's Spirit, and the Scriptures declare that "God is love" (I John 4:16). Therefore, a person who receives the Holy Ghost receives the Spirit of love. However, if that experience is not kept current, the original love will wane.

*Submission.* When we come to God in salvation, we recognize Him as Savior and Lord of our lives. Our will is submitted to His. We want Him to direct our lives.

Each of us has talents and abilities which make us unique persons. And God takes this into consideration in developing a unique plan for each of our lives. Seeking His will, finding and following His plan, will bring about our greatest happiness and resultant good attitude.

*Trust.* To be fully submitted to God, we must trust

Him and believe that He has our best interest at heart. Trust is basic to any love relationship. To love God as He desires, we must trust Him.

When life's difficulties come our way, we can have the proper attitude because we know that whatever comes He can make something good of it. Although we may be unable to see how anything good could possibly come from a particular situation, He can see the future. "And we know that all things work together for good to them that love God, to them who are the called according to his purpose" (Romans 8:28).

Some people may feel hesitant to turn everything over to God, thinking that He might take unfair advantage of them. However, anyone feeling this way has the wrong concept of God. God is not an ogre with a club just waiting to pounce on our possessions. God is loving, gentle, caring, and kind. He wants the best for us. When we turn our lives completely over to Him, He will bless us and make us into something better than we ever thought possible. We can trust Him.

*Praise.* Many verses of Scripture declare that we are to praise God: "It is a good thing to give thanks unto the LORD, and to sing praises unto thy name, O most High" (Psalm 92:1).

Praise has brought dramatic results in seemingly impossible situations, as many people can testify.

In 1977 shortly before Beverly Burk and her husband Dorsey left the United States as missionaries to Germany, she was diagnosed as having granulomatous colitis, also known as Crohn's, an incurable disease as far as medical science was concerned.

In 1980 when she came to the United States for her mother's funeral, she was too ill to return to Germany. Doctors gave her six months to live. Although there were many pain-filled months and the future looked bleak, she learned to respond with *praise*. This was possible because Bev believes that all things work together for good.

When a person is in pain or in a seemingly hopeless situation, he focuses on that. Praise changes the focus from the problem to God. "When you praise, you look at the problem through God," Bev stated. "Praise unties God's hands so He can show you a miracle that He wants to do through that difficult situation."

Bev believes that such praise does not come overnight. One must make a conscious, concerted effort to develop an attitude of praise. In any situation, a Christian can find something for which to praise God. If he cannot use his legs, he can thank God for the use of his arms. A person can begin by praising God for one thing and then expand from there. It is a growing process.

It took seven years, but Bev was eventually able to praise God even for Crohn's disease because through it God brought about some changes she had desired in her attitudes. At some point, she does not know just when, God healed her of Crohn's disease. Her doctor is amazed, but Bev is not. She praised her way through. Although she would not want to repeat the experience, she is thankful for what she learned and for her spiritual growth during that time.

**Attitude Toward Others**

Perhaps the Golden Rule best summarizes what our attitude should be toward others. A paraphrase of Matthew 7:12, the Golden Rule states, "Do unto others as you would have them do unto you." In other words, we should try to put ourselves in the other person's place and act accordingly.

The Apostle Paul said, "By love serve one another.

For all the law is fulfilled in one word, even in this; Thou shalt love thy neighbour as thyself" (Galatians 5:13-14). How can one express the attitude of a servant in love?

*Be compassionate.* According to *Webster's New Collegiate Dictionary,* compassion is a "sympathetic consciousness of others' distress together with a desire to alleviate it." One who has experienced a distressing situation can empathize with another who is going through a similar experience. For example, a person who has lost a loved one knows how another feels in that situation. However, even if one has not been through such an experience, he can attempt to understand by trying to think how he would feel in that situation. Whatever he would like for someone to do for him, he should try to do for the person who needs help.

*Be sensitive.* A person needs to develop a sensitivity to the feelings of others. In her book, *It Takes So Little To Be Above Average,* Florence Littauer tells of some of the insensitive comments unthinking people have made to parents of abnormal children. How could a person be so insensitive as to say, "Look at that ugly baby"?

Even those who want to be kind and considerate often find themselves so busy that they do not take time to minister to the needs of others. Sometimes a person does not express a need directly. We need to "listen between the words" to pick up subtle hints of anxiety, frustration, or depression. Being sensitive to these unspoken feelings will help us meet the needs.

*Be encouraging.* Everyone has times during his life when he needs encouragement. The ability to listen is important in the encouragement process. Giving someone time and attention and making an attempt to understand him, his feelings, and the situation will provide a great relief. We can help him to see the silver lining to his problem cloud, help him to look forward to a bright future, let him know we will stand beside him, encourage him in productive activities.

*Be respectful.* Of course we should respect our leaders and those in authority. (See I Thessalonians 5:12-13.) However, as God's creation, every person should be valued. His feelings, thoughts, and opinions should not be ridiculed, nor should he be made to feel inferior. In talking with another about his problems, we should respect his right to privacy. We can be concerned without prying into areas he is reluctant to discuss.

*Be honest.* Honesty is basic to a lasting relationship. Without it, trust is impossible. This does not mean that we should say everything that comes to mind. For example, telling a lady she needs to lose fifty pounds would not be using wisdom. Even when constructive criticism is in order, it can be given tactfully and still be honest.

*Be positive.* Christians should look for the best in every situation and look for the best in others. Everyone has both faults and strong points. It is up to each individual which he will focus upon. A person who criticizes others and complains continually is not pleasant to be around. However, a person who is sincerely complimentary and points out the good qualities in others is a joy to be with.

Consider Barnabas. When no one else believed in newly-converted Saul (Paul), Barnabas believed in him and recommended him to others in the ministry. What might have happened to Paul if Barnabas had not believed in him?

*Be forgiving.* Since no one on earth is perfect, we can expect to be hurt at some time during the course of life. Whether intentional or unintentional, the situation must be dealt with if we are to keep a right attitude. Holding a grudge will only create anger and bitterness.

Forgiving others is not optional; it is a prerequisite for God's forgiveness to us: "For if ye forgive men their trespasses, your heavenly Father will also forgive you: But if ye forgive not men their trespasses, neither will your Father forgive your trespasses" (Matthew 6:14-15).

Since forgiveness is mandatory, what steps can we take to achieve this sometimes difficult task?

- Realize that no human being is perfect. We all make mistakes.
- Examine the situation to see if we are even remotely at fault. Be honest. If we are at fault, we should ask God to forgive us, and ask the person involved to forgive us.
- Be willing to forgive. If we feel we cannot forgive or really do not want to forgive, we need to ask God to make us willing.
- As an act of his will, not a response to feeling, a person can say (preferably aloud), "I forgive (person's name) for (what hurt him)."
- Pray for the person. This may be difficult at first, but continuing to do so will eventually result in our feelings changing toward him.

*Be thankful.* Someone has said that we should live with an "attitude of gratitude." Not only should we be thankful to God, but we should be thankful toward others. Expressing gratefulness will quickly dispel criticism. When we express thankfulness to someone for something he has done, not only will we make him feel good for having done it, but our own spirit will be lifted.

## Attitude Toward Ourselves

Much has been written about self-esteem, also called self-worth or self-image. A proper self-image is not an egotistical, narcissistic, "holier-than-thou" attitude. It is saying with the Apostle Paul, "I can do all things through Christ which strengtheneth me" (Philippians 4:13).

Self-esteem is the way a person views himself, and it is developed over a period of time. Beginning early in childhood, a person perceives his value through positive or negative feelings determined by the way he views his parents' reaction to him. A child must be disciplined, but the discipline should be given in love.

A positive self-image enables a Christian to live a more effective, productive, successful life for Christ. Such a person will be more willing to be involved in the activities of the church, will be a better witness, and will be able to overcome difficulties more easily.

A person's self-image is the combined product of all experiences and relationships in life up to the present time. Therefore, a person's current self-image does not have to be permanent. By creating experiences generating success and positive relationships, he will improve his self-image and become a happier person.

In *Success Through a Positive Mental Attitude,* authors Napoleon Hill and W. Clement Stone state, "One of the surest ways to find happiness for yourself is to devote your energies toward making someone else happy. Happiness is an elusive, transitory thing. And if you set out to search for it, you will find it evasive. But if you try to bring happiness to someone else, then it comes to you."

Developing a good sense of humor makes for a good attitude. The ability to laugh at one's own mistakes, to see the incongruity in a situation, to see a situation from a humorous standpoint has relieved many a tense moment.

Contentment is important to one's attitude: "But godliness with contentment is great gain" (I

Timothy 6:6). Being discontent with one's physical features, background, abilities, or status in life can create a poor self-image. Comparing ourselves with others can make us feel inferior. The Bible says, "But they measuring themselves by themselves, and comparing themselves among themselves, are not wise" (II Corinthians 10:12).

A person should examine himself to find if some things he sees as undesirable can be changed. For example, if he thinks his hair style is unbecoming, perhaps he can find a more flattering style. If he would like to have a better job, he might take adult education classes to improve his qualifications. However, some things cannot be changed and should be accepted.

Wishing for something that is impossible can only lead to frustration and self-pity. The young man who is 5'6" cannot become 6'4" by any amount of wishing. If that height is not programmed into his genes, wishing he were tall is an exercise in futility. Comparing himself unfavorably to his tall buddies will create self-pity as well as develop a poor self-image.

Just as one's negative thoughts about himself develop a poor self-image, positive thoughts help develop a good self-image.

*Imaging* is a term used by Norman Vincent Peale and others to describe a mental procedure of picturing in one's mind a vivid image of a desired outcome. According to Peale, imaging is most effective "when it is combined with a strong religious faith, backed by prayer and the seemingly illogical technique of giving thanks for benefits before they are received." He believes that if this process is used consistently over a period of time, "it solves problems, strengthens personalities, improves health, and greatly enhances the chances for success in any kind of endeavor."

This concept is based on an interpretation of Jesus' statement, "What things soever ye desire, when ye pray, believe that ye receive them, and ye shall have them" (Mark 11:24). It is perceived as an act of faith; for if one believes that a certain thing will happen, he can see it in his mind's eye.

Seeing oneself as having a positive attitude will help to bring it about. A Christian should realize that he is a child of God, made in His image. By developing a right relationship with God, he will be able to reach out to others with a proper attitude. This will in turn help to improve his self-image which will result in greater happiness.

Attitude is the key. As Alfred A. Montapert has said, "Have a happy, loving attitude. A positive attitude is mature health. This is the best state of psychological and spiritual health that can be obtained on this earth. Happiness depends not on things around me, but on my attitude. Everything in my life will depend on my attitude."

## Test Your Knowledge

1. A person will see problems and difficulties either as stumbling blocks or as _____ _____. His _____ determines how he views problems.

2. _____ is important in every area of a person's life.

3. Three areas of relationships where one's attitude is very important are his relationship with _____, _____, and _____.

4. A Christian can only be truly happy and possess a positive attitude when he is in the _____ _____ _____.

5. _____ God changes the focal point of our attention from our problems to the greatness of God.

17

6. The _____ _____ summarizes well what our attitude should be toward others.

7. _____ others is a prerequisite to obtaining the forgiveness of God.

8. Self-esteem is the way a person views _____.

9. A proper self-image includes acknowledging the power of _____ in one's life.

10. Happiness does not depend on a person's circumstances, but rather on his _____.

## Apply Your Knowledge

How is your attitude? You may try this simple project to analyze your attitude and observe the effect it bears on your emotions and overall happiness.

Create a small, personal diary or log book which you can carry with you each day. It might include the following headings: problem, immediate response, action initiated, delayed response, effect on mood and attitude, overall effectiveness throughout the day.

Recording information under these headings will do a couple of things for you. First, it will help you evaluate yourself—weaknesses, strengths, failures and successes. Secondly, it will elevate your general awareness of your attitude, hence helping you to adjust it before it creates even greater problems.

If bad habits can be made, good habits can also be formed. As you carry this diary with you, it will become a habit, urging you to guard your attitude.

## Expand Your Knowledge

Before reading chapter two of *Spiritual Growth and Maturity*, read I Samuel 24. You will find there a beautiful background story concerning loyalty. Loyalty is a sure step toward true spiritual maturity.

# Loyalty—The Way of a Godly Life

*If therefore ye have not been faithful in the unrighteous mammon, who will commit to your trust the true riches?*

*Luke 16:11*

---

**Start With the Scriptures**

I Samuel 22
II Samuel 2
Matthew 25:14-30
Luke 12:35-40

I Timothy 6:1-2
II Timothy 2:2
I Corinthians 4:2

---

### God Rewards Loyalty

In the parable of the talents (Matthew 25:14-30), Jesus plainly demonstrated that while God rewards loyalty and faithfulness to the gifts and callings He has given His people, He also brings harsh judgment upon those who treat them indifferently. And rightly so, when we consider the great price He paid not only to give us eternal life but also to enable us, with these gifts, to do the work of His kingdom.

God has given us precious gifts at the expense of His own life's blood. He has not withheld anything from us, but He has freely given us His gifts. He has lavished them upon all who have been born of His Spirit. "But unto every one of us is given grace according to the measure of the gift of Christ" (Ephesians 4:7).

The Apostle Paul continued by writing that these gifts so freely provided by Christ were purchased at great cost. He was crucified for us, descended into the lower parts of the earth, and ascended into Heaven that He might provide all the gifts and offices necessary "for the perfecting of the saints, for the work of the ministry" (Ephesians 4:12).

Sometimes people fail to properly value a gift. If a person must work hard and sacrifice in order to obtain something he desperately wants, he tends to place a premium on its value. However, if it is given to him, he may value it much less. At times God's people act like spoiled children who have been showered with gifts. They treat them like playthings, picking them up and laying them down, giving little thought to their true worth.

Jesus warned that His priceless gifts are not playthings. These gifts are freely given to His children but they are also accountable to Him for their disposition. Being faithful means being trustworthy. Since Christians have been entrusted with the most precious gifts, they cannot violate that trust without being held responsible.

The Apostle Paul wrote, "Moreover it is required in stewards, that a man be found faithful" (I Corinthians 4:2). A steward must be trustworthy. He must be loyal to his master and to his calling. He cannot remain a steward if he is slothful and indifferent.

In the parable cited above, Jesus told the story of a certain master who called three of his servants and distributed his goods to them.

He entrusted them with his money and gave them the opportunity to do whatever they desired. If they chose to waste it, they could, but one day he would return to demand an accounting of their stewardship. They possibly knew he would be gone for a considerable time, so they might have been lulled into believing they would have ample opportunity to get their affairs in order before he returned.

The master gave each of his servants different amounts of money. We are not told what the talents were. If they were gold, for example, each talent would be valued at about $1,000,000 at today's rates.

Some people excuse their lack of commitment by saying that if God had given them more ability, they would be able to be useful in His kingdom but, after all, what can they do? It is not ours to question His distribution of gifts. He gives to every man according to his ability. He does not require a person to go beyond his capabilities. On the other hand, He does not give a person less than he is able to handle.

While the master was gone, two of the servants began working with the money they had received. They carefully invested it in various enterprises, and with responsible management, watched their investment grow. The servant who had received five talents had more to work with. Hence, he was able to gain another five. The servant who had received two, gained two more. Each had doubled his investment by the time his master returned. The third servant, however, did nothing. He simply hid his master's money in the ground and waited. Waited for what? For the right opportunity to come along? For someone else to do the work for him? He was afraid he might make a mistake, so he did nothing.

Can it be said that the servant who hid his master's money, buried it in himself? Does it really matter what I do with the gift(s) the Lord has given me? Am I responsible to do something significant in His kingdom? Will He accept the excuse, "I just never got around to doing anything. After all, I was so busy with my own life and my plans I didn't have any time"?

When the master returned he demanded an accounting from each servant. The two who were faithful received the same commendation. He did not commend the one who had gained five talents more than the one who had gained two. Each had done his best and each was accordingly commended. "Well done, thou good and faithful servant: thou hast been faithful over a few things, I will make thee ruler over many things: enter thou into the joy of thy lord" (Matthew 25:21).

We cannot have the responsibility of great things given to us until we have proven faithful in lesser things. A young man may aspire to the ministry and desire to be the pastor of a thriving church, but he will not achieve his goal if he fails to be faithful in his local church in lesser responsibilities.

The third servant attempted to excuse his slothfulness by telling his master, "I was afraid, and went and hid thy talent in the earth" (verse 25). To this feeble excuse, his lord thundered, "Thou wicked and slothful servant" (verse 26). The angry lord then ordered the man to be cast into outer darkness where there shall be weeping and gnashing of teeth. There was no acceptable excuse for the person who did nothing with the gift the master had given him.

**From Rags to Riches**

When the Lord saves people from sin, He calls them out of darkness and brings them into His marvelous light. They are made new creatures in Christ. The old life, with its attendant miseries, is replaced with a life of peace and joy in the Holy Ghost.

We have been entrusted with so much. Even the angels have not been given the gifts entrusted to the church. We are the sons of God. "Unto which of the angels said he at any time, Thou art my Son, this day have I begotten thee?" (Hebrews 1:5). "Are they not all ministering spirits, sent forth to minister for them who shall be heirs of salvation?" (Hebrews 1:14). "Unto us they [the prophets] did minister the things, which are now reported unto you by them that have preached the gospel unto you with the Holy Ghost sent down from heaven; which things the angels desire to look into" (I Peter 1:12).

The Apostle Paul cried, "O the depth of the riches both of the wisdom and knowledge of God!" (Romans 11:33). And again, "That ye may know what is the hope of his calling, and what the riches of the glory of his inheritance in the saints, And what is the exceeding greatness of his power to us-ward who believe, according to the working of his mighty power" (Ephesians 1:18-19).

Indeed, Christians are rich! But with these great riches, freely given us by Christ, comes tremendous responsibility. We are stewards of far greater treasures than silver and gold. Jesus said, "If therefore ye have not been faithful in the unrighteous mammon, who will commit to your trust the true riches? And if ye have not been faithful in that which is another man's, who shall give you that which is your own?" (Luke 16:11-12). The mammon Jesus spoke of is money or material goods. If we cannot be trusted to give God that which belongs to Him and use our material blessings in a way that glorifies Him, how can we be entrusted with His spiritual gifts?

## David Exemplified Loyalty

The life of David demonstrates how a young man ultimately became king after years of walking with

God and being faithful to every responsibility given him, regardless of how insignificant it may have appeared to others. He was faithful to God, faithful to his father, faithful to his task, faithful to King Saul, and faithful in leadership.

David learned some valuable lessons in his early years. The long days and nights spent alone caring for his father's sheep were important foundation stones in the development of his character. Rather than looking with disdain upon this simple task, he carefully studied the ways of sheep and learned valuable lessons that would one day provide him insight in leading people. He did not think himself ill used because he was forced to be separated from his family and friends. He took time to worship his God. He expressed his love to Him in song and in praise. The Book of Psalms abounds with these deep expressions from this great man's heart.

David learned to trust God for help in times of trouble. There was no one else in those lonely hills to help him when a bear or lion snatched an unsuspecting lamb. His strength was no match for these beasts but, in his time of need, he cried to the Lord and received divine intervention.

Later, when all Israel trembled before the giant Goliath, he told King Saul, "Thy servant kept his father's sheep, and there came a lion, and a bear, and took a lamb out of the flock: And I went out after him, and smote him, and delivered it out of his mouth: and when he arose against me, I caught him by his beard, and smote him, and slew him. Thy servant slew both the lion and the bear: and this uncircumcised Philistine shall be as one of them, seeing he hath defied the armies of the living God" (I Samuel 17:34-36).

Years later he would be able to reflect back again and again to those times and strengthen himself in the Lord as he faced impossible odds. It was through such tests of faith that he penned the immortal promises which have sustained God's people over the years. He encouraged others to trust the Lord as their Good Shepherd (Psalm 23).

David's older brothers scoffed at his faith in God. What did he know about fighting battles? He wasn't a soldier; he was a mere shepherd boy. His father had sent him to his three brothers with food for them and their captains. When David arrived, he heard Goliath's challenge and was amazed that no one would meet him on the battlefield. After all, "Who is this uncircumcised Philistine, that he should defy the armies of the living God?" (I Samuel 17:26). At this, his eldest brother, Eliab, chided him: "Eliab's anger was kindled against David, and he said, Why camest thou down hither? and with whom hast thou left those few sheep in the wilderness?" (verse 28).

David's loyalty to God, his father, and to his task prevented him from being a self-seeking person. He had no thought of confronting the giant to gain personal recognition; he had no aspirations for self aggrandizement. David was a kingdom-minded man. His first consideration was the kingdom. To his brother's rebuke he replied, "Is there not a cause?"

A mighty victory was won that day by a young man who was totally dedicated to the cause of God and who believed his God would bring deliverance to those who would dare step out in faith.

There is a great cause at stake in the kingdom of God. What a difference it makes when each Christian sees the greater "cause" of the kingdom of God and is not concerned about promoting himself and his own personal causes.

Jonathan, Saul's son and apparent heir to the throne, admired the qualities he saw in young David: "The soul of Jonathan was knit with the soul of David, and Jonathan loved him as his own soul" (I Samuel 18:1).

Saul, on the other hand, soon became insanely jealous of David. All Israel rejoiced over the great victory God had given. As the women sang David's praises, Saul seethed in anger. Soon he was trying to spear David to the wall during his frequent fits of rage: "Saul was afraid of David, because the LORD was with him, and was departed from Saul" (I Samuel 18:12).

The once great leader of Israel was so consumed with jealousy that he wanted to destroy the man whom God had used to bring deliverance. David, however, made no attempt to hurt Saul. Quite to the contrary, he did everything he could to help him. When the evil spirit came upon the tormented king, it was David who played his harp and sang, trying to soothe the king's troubled mind.

Saul's paranoia drove him to deeper and deeper extremes as he tried repeatedly to kill David. Finally, David fled for his life. His high principles of moral integrity would not allow him to lift a finger against Saul even though he knew the king was wrong.

Keenly aware of Saul's viciousness, David went to the king of Moab and requested permission for his mother and father to live there. Once his parents were safely settled, David returned to his beloved land only to be hunted like a common criminal.

As Saul pursued David, he came to Gibeah and there set up camp. As Saul's men gathered around him, he bemoaned his fate and chided them for conspiring against him and being in league with David. He whined, "There is none of you that is sorry for me" (I Samuel 22:8). To him, everyone was sympathetic to David; no one cared for him. He even insulted his own loyal son because he was David's friend.

While Saul was encamped at Gibeah, Doeg the Edomite reported that he had been present at the Tabernacle when the high priest had given David and his men the showbread to eat, along with Goliath's sword. Saul's distorted mind could not see this as an act of kindness on the part of the priests. To him, it was just another indication of a growing conspiracy that must be stamped out. Immediately he ordered the high priest brought before him to give account for this act of treason.

Ahimelech, the high priest, could hardly comprehend Saul's anger: "Who is so faithful among all thy servants as David, which is the king's son in law, and goeth at thy bidding, and is honourable in thine house?" (I Samuel 22:14). This was evidently the general consensus of opinion among the people of Israel. But his words fell on deaf ears; they could not penetrate the hardened spirit that only sought vengeance.

Saul's wickedness now drove him to do the unpardonable, to strike out at God by killing His priests. He ordered his soldiers to kill Ahimelech and the priests with him, but the soldiers stood immobile in shocked silence. No one would lift a finger against God's priests. Saul then turned to Doeg to carry out the slaughter of these innocent men, and he gladly complied.

Doeg would do anything to ingratiate himself to Saul. He lived by one principle—the principle of self-preservation. With no compunction, he killed all eighty-five priests, their wives and children, and destroyed their city.

Still Saul hounded David. When he heard that David was hiding in the wilderness of Engedi, he took 3,000 men with him to assure his prey would not escape. One night he and his men found shelter in a cave and were soon asleep. Little did they suspect that David and his men were hiding in the sides of that very cave.

When David's men saw Saul and his men lie down, they urged David to kill him. Surely, they argued,

God has finally put this evil man in your hands. David stole silently to Saul and cut off part of his robe. When he returned to his men, he felt he had wronged Saul. His conscience immediately smote him. He had dared to cut off part of his king's garment.

David confessed to his men that he could not hurt Saul; the king was the Lord's anointed. Later, David cried out to Saul and when Saul looked behind him, David was bowing in obeisance (prostrating himself on the ground!). Saul was so moved by David's great act of kindness in sparing his life that he wept and he, too, admitted to David's unswerving loyalty.

"And he said to David, Thou art more righteous than I: for thou hast rewarded me good, whereas I have rewarded thee evil. And thou hast shewed this day how that thou hast dealt well with me: forasmuch as when the LORD had delivered me into thine hand, thou killedst me not. For if a man find his enemy, will he let him go well away? wherefore the LORD reward thee good for that thou hast done unto me this day. And now, behold, I know well that thou shalt surely be king, and that the kingdom of Israel shall be established in thine hand" (I Samuel 24:17-20).

Saul soon recovered from his remorse and again relentlessly pursued David. After he and his men had set up camp, they lay down to sleep.

David took Abishai with him to steal down to Saul's camp. Abishai assured David that God had indeed delivered Saul into his hand this time and begged David to permit him to kill the king. David refused his request on the grounds that Saul was God's anointed; he would leave Saul's judgment in God's hands.

Saul was finally killed in battle and David did become king. As David had loved and trusted his men whom he had led during those long months in the wilderness, so he loved the people of Israel God entrusted to his care. He had survived many bitter disappointments but, even in times of despair, God had helped him.

It was under David's leadership that Israel finally conquered the land God had promised to Abraham. It was through his generosity that great hoards of gold, silver, and brass were appropriated for the building of the Temple. David could have kept all these spoils of battle for himself, but he willingly dedicated them to the God he so deeply loved.

Jesus taught that one reaps what he sows. David was faithful to God, to his father, to his task, to Saul, and to his people. Consequently, God surrounded him with faithful men who admired and respected him. He did not have to demand respect from his people; he received their love and respect because of the man he was, not because of the position he held.

It will be worth every sacrifice and inconvenience to hear the Master say, "Well done, thou good and faithful servant: thou hast been faithful over a few things, I will make thee ruler over many things: enter thou into the joy of thy lord."

## Test Your Knowledge

### True or False

_____ 1. While the parable of the talents demonstrates that God rewards loyalty and faithfulness, it also reveals that God will judge those who are disloyal and unfaithful.

_____ 2. Being faithful means being trustworthy.

_____ 3. A Christian can still remain a steward of Jesus Christ even though he may be slothful and indifferent.

_____ 4. Even the angels have not been given the gifts that have been given to the church.

_____ 5. David was loyal to almost everyone except his father.

_____ 6. David was a kingdom-minded person—not self-seeking.

_____ 7. David would have slain Saul had the opportunity ever arisen.

_____ 8. Saul was not loyal to David.

_____ 9. David told Saul, "Thou art more righteous than I."

\_\_\_\_\_10. David's loyalty paid off in part when he became the king of Israel.

## Applying Your Knowledge

Loyalty is actually unconditional love. Christ was loyal to the church through Calvary. We should be loyal to Him through our service.

You might want to set some goals of loyalty for yourself. Some of the target areas should be loyalty to our parents, God, pastor, superiors at work, governmental officials and friends. Our goal should be complete loyalty to these individuals in our lives, regardless of external circumstances. "A friend loveth at all times" (Proverbs 17:17). That is true loyalty.

## Expand Your Knowledge

Read and study the Scriptures for the next chapter before continuing. These will prepare a proper foundation for the chapter itself.

It would be good also to read one of E. M. Bounds' books on prayer such as *Power Through Prayer*. They are easy reading and will bless you with many fundamental thoughts on prayer.

# Teach Us to Pray

*And it came to pass, that, as he was praying in a certain place, when he ceased, one of his disciples said unto him, Lord, teach us to pray, as John also taught his disciples.*

*Luke 11:1*

---

**Start With the Scriptures**

| | |
|---|---|
| II Chronicles 7:14 | Ephesians 6:18 |
| Psalm 145:18 | I Thessalonians 5:17 |
| Matthew 7:7-8 | I Timothy 2:8 |
| Luke 11:1-13; 18:1 | Hebrews 4:16 |
| Romans 8:26 | James 5:16 |
| I Corinthians 14:15 | Jude 20 |

---

Prayer is life's limitless contact with the power of God. Jesus lived in a dimension of intimacy with power and limitlessness that caused wonder in the minds of the masses. This created a desire for the same intimacy in the hearts of His disciples: "And it came to pass, that, as he was praying in a certain place, when he ceased, one of his disciples said unto him, Lord, teach us to pray" (Luke 11:1).

This was an interesting request. Had the disciples not prayed? Surely they had, but the disciple who asked this question evidently recognized a communication and power not evident in the type of praying that he had learned from his father in the synagogue. Jesus was praying—not just saying prayers. A spiritual exchange was evident that aroused this disciple to say, "Lord, teach me how to do that." He had caught sight of Christ's limitless reach in prayer.

Jesus did not teach His disciples to pray until they asked. Their prayers of petition, thanksgiving, and praise were basically one-way prayers. But when Jesus prayed there was a two-way flow of power. The Christ, who limited Himself for our salvation, drew power and direction from the unlimited strength and mind of God.

Praying is similar to creating a vacuum. All the forces of the universe flow to fill a vacuum of life and restore balance and harmony in response to prayer. So it was with Christ's prayers. He created a vacuum in His compassion and intercession for men. The power and resources of God's universe were acquired and appropriated to meet man's need. "Lord, teach us to pray!"

## Principles of Prayer

In response to the request, Jesus gave an example of prayer that set forth the essential principles. (See Luke 11:1-13.) The disciples did not use it as one more chant to add to their repertoire. This prayer speaks to the spiritual and the natural factors of which our lives consist. But what are the dynamics of prayer?

*Prayer from God's kingdom perspective.* From "Our Father" to "Thy will be done, as in heaven, so in earth" sets the perspective from which Christians should pray. Such a perspective opens one's horizons and causes him to think like God thinks. A person moves from his little corner of the world and from his favorite place of prayer into the mind, the thoughts, and the will of God. It is only from this vantage point that a Christian can see his true needs and honestly evaluate his petitions. From the kingdom perspective, "the things of earth will grow strangely dim in the light of His glory and grace."

But things of this earth *do* matter, and there is room for them in prayer.

*Trust the Lord's generosity toward human need.* "Give us day by day our daily bread." The Lord does not wait for a spectacular moment to display His graciousness. He provides the most mundane need of ordinary, daily living—bread. The mundane, however, is often the most necessary to life. God is concerned with our daily needs.

What is too small, too ordinary to mention? Discounting God's involvement in the mundane needs of life only limits Him.

*Trust His commitment to our salvation.* "And forgive us our sins. . . .And lead us not into temptation; but deliver us from evil." His work in our behalf is complete. He forgives, guides and delivers. Is there a spiritual problem that falls outside of this provision? Not one!

Before looking at other principles of prayer taught in this chapter, the balance of the whole prayer should be considered. The greater part of the prayer is acknowledging God's perspective. The next largest portion relates to our eternal well-being, and the smallest portion has to do with our physical welfare.

It is not more difficult for God to deliver one from evil than for Him to help that person pay his taxes. Perhaps the petition for physical needs appears first because without those provisions the spiritual needs multiply. The kingdom perspective makes provision for the whole man: "But seek ye first the kingdom of God, and his righteousness; and all these things shall be added unto you" (Matthew 6:33).

*Overcome indifference with persistence.* Jesus told of a sleepy neighbor whose friend sought some bread at midnight (Luke 11:5). A similar story was related concerning an unjust judge. (See Luke 18:1-8.) In both stories the common denominator was the need of persistence.

The Lord is not as a sleepy friend or an unjust judge, but sometimes Christians are. The heart-felt needs of the world knock on their doors so persistently that they almost cease to hear them. Selfish, apathetic and unjust spirits can arise within Christians to hinder their prayers.

There is a need for a holy stubbornness— persistence. In this day of instant solutions, most people find this one of the most difficult and frustrating kinds of prayer. But there are some needs that will never be met until Christians engage themselves in insistent, persistent, aggressive prayer.

One must keep praying and not faint, for apathy and indifference are not immovable objects in the face of the irresistible force of prayer. Nothing moved, in either of the recorded accounts, until prayer created a force that overcame the inertia of apathy. It was for self-interest that the friend got up and provided bread. He wanted to sleep. It was for purely selfish motives that the judge moved to avenge the woman of her enemies. He was tired of the hassle. God did not suddenly make them kind and unselfish, but He used their evil to bring good to the petitioner.

In sharp contrast to such uncaring, uninterested men is the deeply unselfish heart of the Lord. He sees the sparrow that falls. He can surely be moved by the feelings of one's infirmities when that person is persistent in prayer.

*Be direct and specific in your approach.* If a Christian has a question—he should ask. If you need help—ask. Sometimes individuals do without because they have not asked. A person may pour his energy into making the impossible dream a reality then wonder why he suffers from burnout. Every dream that God births into our spirits is an impossible dream unless He is actively involved. A person may know the will of God and what he should do. He sets himself wholly to the task only to find the task will destroy him unless he acknowledges his dependency on God—by asking. A Christian's consistent asking is an affirmation of his true humility and a confirmation of his trust in the living Lord.

*If something has been lost—seek after it.* Through a lifetime of serving the Lord, a person is given many gifts and benefits. But sometimes they become lost by neglect or by not understanding their value; sometimes they are stolen. Sometimes, for example, Satan may steal one's joy. Joy belongs to God's children; it is part of the kingdom of God that is given by the Holy Spirit. A person can endeavor to live a long and productive Christian life without experiencing the deep, rich power of joy, but why should he just accept the loss? He should seek it in prayer.

*When the door is closed—knock.* There is no room that Jesus Christ cannot enter, nor is there a door He cannot open. The only door He stands on the outside of is the door of one's heart until he opens it to the Lord.

If a person has prepared himself for the "big break" on his job, he should start knocking on the door in prayer. Jesus is ready to open every door when it is in accordance with His will and purpose. There are times He holds the door for our own benefit. Only Jesus really knows what is behind every door of life.

*Accept His answer without fear.* "If a son shall ask bread of any of you that is a father. . . ." Christians can ask freely because they have "father insurance." No request is safer than the request made to a loving father. Children have confidence when they approach their father. This is not presumptuous. "For we have not an high priest which cannot be touched with the feeling of our infirmities. . .*Let us therefore come boldly* unto the throne of grace" (Hebrews 4:15, 16).

One should be ready to accept what God gives him. He should immediately appropriate the things which are given to him since the Lord seldom grants a petition before the hour it is needed.

This principle may not always be easy to apply in the spiritual sense, but seeking spiritual power outside of Jesus Christ is spiritual suicide. To ask the Father for His Spirit, His power, and indwelling presence, is to receive life.

Earthly fathers, although loving, may have their judgment distorted by evil. In contrast, our Heavenly Father loves us and knows what is right. We can trust God when His answer is no. Because we can trust Him, we have a greater freedom to ask.

A good editor frees a writer to write with greater liberty. The writer knows the editor will prune away ideas that are weak or misleading.

Other principles of prayer are recorded like "gold nuggets" throughout the Bible. As they are practiced, one's prayer life can become a life of power.

## Praying Beyond Ourselves

The Apostle Paul introduced a dimension of prayer that the disciples could not have understood at the time of Jesus' teaching about prayer. The Holy Spirit had not yet been poured out. Paul wrote about praying in the dimension of the Spirit. This is possible only through the indwelling power of the Holy Spirit.

"Likewise the Spirit also helpeth our infirmities: for we know not what we should pray for as we ought" (Romans 8:26). Sometimes Christians do not know what to pray for or how to pray, but the Spirit does. "He that searcheth the hearts knoweth what is the mind of the Spirit" (Romans 8:27). The Holy Spirit that searches the hearts of all men knows the mind and will of God.

It is the Holy Ghost that prays through a child of God, making intercession with groanings that cannot be verbalized with words. As we give ourselves to this kind of prayer, the Holy Spirit becomes the One who prays, the intercessor, through the vehicle of our flesh. We are in partnership with the Holy Spirit in matters beyond our human strength and understanding.

What is a Christian's responsibility? As he enters into prayer he might or might not understand intellectually the subject of his intercession. Nonetheless, he should willingly yield himself to the cause and to the inexpressible flow of the Holy Spirit. The heart must be open to the searching of the Spirit, because searching and interceding go hand in hand.

## Purpose of Prayer

What is the purpose of such praying in the Spirit? *There is a productive travail, like a woman in labor, that produces new babes into the kingdom of God.* This kind of travail may be evident before the birth of a new church, a Bible school, a new outreach, or a consecration to the ministry. There are often visible results of such prayers.

*There is also praying in the Holy Ghost which builds up one's own spirit.* (See Jude 20.) It provides strength and courage which is unavailable by any other means. "That he would grant you. . .to be strengthened with might by his Spirit in the inner man" (Ephesians 3:16).

*Prayer may equip a Christian for spiritual warfare.* "Put on the whole armour of God. . .For we wrestle not against flesh and blood" (Ephesians 6:11, 12). There is a spiritual warfare being waged and prayer is a vital part of the Christian's armor. "Praying always with all prayer and supplication in the Spirit, and watching thereunto with all perseverance and supplication for all saints" (Ephesians 6:18). Our King may be preparing a soldier for battle through prayer in the Spirit.

*Praying in the Spirit may bring insight and knowledge to one's mind.* He may not understand fully the burden of the Spirit when he enters into prayer, but as he prays God begins to focus his attention on a specific matter.

"Wherefore let him that speaketh in an unknown tongue pray that he may interpret. For if I pray in an unknown tongue, my spirit prayeth, but my understanding is unfruitful" (I Corinthians 14:13-14). It is the will of God that a Christian's understanding should be enlightened—if not immediately, at least ultimately. This is why we should pray for the interpretation of utterances given in tongues.

Paul's testimony to the Corinthians was, "I will pray with the spirit, and I will pray with the understanding also: I will sing with the spirit, and I will sing with the understanding also" (I Corinthians 14:15).

## The Practice of Prayer

Prayer is a communication skill. Communication skills, such as speaking, singing and writing are learned primarily by doing and secondarily by study.

Power in prayer begins with the practice of praying. As one prays, he learns the language of prayer.

It is enjoyable to listen to a baby as it begins to imitate sounds. Over and over come the soft sounds of "bah-bah, bah-bah." We listen with delight to hear that first "da-da." Usually "ma-ma" soon follows. They experience their amazing power to bring pleasure to their parents with these two words. Soon comes the powerful word of control, "no." How well and how often they use it.

A Christian's beginning prayers may be quite infantile, but the first cry of "Abba, Father" (like a child crying "daddy"), with arms extended heavenward, are a great delight to the Heavenly Father. All too quickly one passes to the stage of giving orders from his want list and trying to control his world with prayer. But God has called us to maturity.

Specific times for prayer are important in establishing a spiritual rhythm. Regular times of prayer can be built into the day's schedule just like work, meal, and bed time. Daniel was a prime example of this kind of praying. He had a "three-times-a-day" schedule which he held inviolable, even in the face of the king's decree.

A Christian should find a place of retreat in his home, office or school. Prayer does not necessarily involve a long period of time. It may be only a moment of relaxation and praise in the presence of the Lord, but it can be so refreshing to the soul.

*Morning prayer.* Many great Christian leaders follow the psalmist David's example: "My voice shalt thou hear in the morning, O LORD; in the morning will I direct my prayer unto thee" (Psalm 5:3). There is much to be said in favor of early morning prayer. The body is relaxed and the mind is receptive to the good things of the Lord.

One should awaken his spirit with praise and

thanksgiving before beginning to make petition for his needs. "Be careful (anxious) for nothing; but in every thing by prayer and supplication with thanksgiving let your requests be made known unto God" (Philippians 4:6).

It may help to have a list of needs that should be remembered before the Lord. Prayer can be offered for those in your household, those who have authority over you and those over whom you have authority. Follow earnestly any burden the Lord may quicken to you, but do not stop there.

Time should be left to sit quietly at the feet of Jesus. The day should be committed to Him. The Lord should be allowed to adjust one's priorities, insert new ones that are important to Him, and delete the unimportant. Fifteen minutes of time spent in such a manner may save hours later in the day.

*Continual prayer.* "Pray without ceasing" was Paul's instruction to the Thessalonians (I Thessalonians 5:17). They did not interpret this to mean they should spend twenty-four hours a day on their knees, but rather that they should weave prayer into the fabric of their lives. One should continue in an attitude of prayer. As the Lord brings things to our spiritual attention, we should pray for them immediately. We might not have the opportunity to drop to our knees but we can carry that person or need to the Lord in prayer.

Little incidents that prick our spiritual awareness are like small grains of sand in the shell of the oyster. They can be coated with prayer and made into something precious when they would otherwise be an uncomfortable irritant.

## The Impact of Prayer

To study the impact of prayer would be to study the text of the entire Bible. One fact is evident:

prayer has both personal and national impact. Evidence of the person-to-person impact of prayer was demonstrated in the words of James 5:14-16: "Is any sick among you? let him call for the elders of the church; and let them pray...And the prayer of faith shall save the sick." This prayer brings healing to the body. But the text said further, "And if he have committed sins, they shall be forgiven him. Confess your faults one to another, and pray one for another, that ye may be healed." Here is forgiveness of sins and healing for the inner man. The total man is touched by prayer.

"The effectual fervent prayer of a righteous man availeth much" (James 5:16). It matters who prays and how fervently the prayer is made. The righteous man, praying with great fervor, can create a powerful "vacuum" that attracts Heaven's resources. Jesus, the truly righteous One, prayed for us in the hour of His greatest passion. We are the fruit of His travail!

Prayer moves the arm that moves the world. "If my people, which are called by my name, shall humble themselves, and pray, and seek my face, and turn from their wicked ways; then will I hear from heaven, and will forgive their sin, and will heal their land" (II Chronicles 7:14). Nations bend to the influence of corporate prayer.

A church once had a Scripture text on a deep blue poster over the prayer-room door. The silver glitter displayed these words:

**Much prayer, Much power;**
**Little prayer, Little power;**
**No prayer, No power.**

The truth of that motto remains, for nothing lies beyond the reach of prayer except that which lies outside the will of God.

## Test Your Knowledge

1. The disciples requested for Jesus to teach them to _____.
2. When Jesus prayed, it was evident there was a two-way flow of _____.
3. We must learn to overcome indifference with _____.
4. We should approach God as children approach their _____.
5. There is a dimension of prayer where Christians learn to pray _____ themselves.
6. The Spirit helps our _____.
7. Praying in the _____ builds up one's own spirit.
8. Prayer equips a Christian for _____.
9. Power in prayer begins with the _____ of praying.
10. Specific _____ for prayer are important.

## Apply Your Knowledge

God answers prayer! If you are not already doing so, try making a prayer chart to keep in your place of prayer. As the various needs are met and prayers answered, scratch the requests off and write down the dates that they are answered.

Nothing builds faith like seeing what God has already done. As you pray each day and see your answered prayers on the chart, you will receive more faith for the present requests.

## Expand Your Knowledge

Read the Scriptures for the following chapter on love. This is an area where Christians should always grow and develop. It is by love that we are known as Christ's disciples.

# The Spectrum of God's Love

*And now abideth faith, hope, charity, these three; but the greatest of these is charity.*

I Corinthians 13:13

---

### Start With the Scriptures

Deuteronomy 11:1
Psalm 91:14
Romans 5:5

Philippians 1:9
II Timothy 1:7
I John 3:17-18; 4:12-21

---

Living without knowing God's love is merely existing as in a desolate wasteland! Life is given a purpose and meaning when the pure life-giving waters of His love flow into the soul.

God's wondrous love defies description. If we read the hundreds of books written about it, sang all the songs with it as their theme, recited all the poems glorifying it and studied all that philosophers have concluded concerning it, we would still not be able to define it. To know God is to know love, for "He is love" (I John 4:8).

George Sweeting wrote:
*"God is the source of love*
*Christ is the proof of love*
*Service is the expression of love*
*Boldness is the outcome of love."*

*Webster's Twentieth Century Dictionary* uses the same word to define "a strong affection, a liking for sexual passion, Cupid, romance, a score in tennis and God's benevolent concern for mankind." Love is probably the word most "used" and "abused."

A dry, thirsty world cries out for the reality of love to meet their needs, for there is a thirst for God within every person that can never be satisfied by drinking from the polluted, muddy waterholes of materialism, professionalism, and intellectualism! "There is a God-shaped vacuum in every heart," wrote Blaise Pascal.

God's love is neither a theory nor mere sentimentality; it is *reality* and meets the needs in all areas of everyday living. Life without His love is a failure because love *is* the life of God!

## A Need To Be Loved

*Marasmus* (wasting away) is a disease among children that does not permit a child to develop socially, psychologically or physically, and the victim usually wastes away and dies! It is not caused by the lack of food or care but by the lack of being loved, and is prevalent in orphanages when babies are not held, kissed, hugged and talked to.

People never outgrow their need to be loved, and as they develop, there is a need for expressed love as well as the need for physical love. God knew that material things could not fulfill the need of love deep within men and did not intend that they should waste away. His love pours into the deep crevices of our minds and souls, and His warm tender touch nourishes us abundantly as He continuously expresses His love for us.

Solomon expressed God's love when he wrote, "He brought me to the banqueting house, and his banner over me was love" (Song of Solomon 2:4). This was the hall where the most precious possessions were kept! Here the wine was preserved by the ancients, and the treasures of brass and polished gold were secluded. His precious possessions were taken here, and love spread a "lavish smorgasbord" before them, providing for them every facet of their needs.

Under His protection, the torment of fear cannot exist, and tribulation, distress, persecution, famine, nakedness, peril or sword cannot destroy love's protective power. For death, life, angels, principalities, powers, things present, things to come, height, depth, or any creature shall not be able to separate us from His love (Romans 8:35-39). The erosion of time cannot diminish the "sameness" of His love; it will never fail, wither, fade away, or become obsolete!

The Apostle Paul emphasized that no matter what one may excel in, it is of no value without love (I Corinthians 13:1-3). Without love as the "conductor" in the use of highly prized gifts, there can be no melody or orchestration—only blaring hollow brass and the crashing of tuneless cymbals! Love—the greatest gift—is compared with the gifts of speech, prophecy, faith, benevolence and martyrdom!

Three words in the Greek language define three dimensions of love. *Eros* is an egocentric, self-gratifying physical expression, and without help it dies or destroys. *Phileo* is the common word for affection in relationships and brings much of the happiness in people's lives. It must have help, or it brings heartbreak, for it dies if it does not receive encouragement. It is withdrawn if the "performance" does not meet its expectations.

Somehow it has been falsely ingrained into many Christians that God loves them according to their performance. Children learn Mommy and Daddy love them "if" they are good; the school teacher loves "good" students; God gives His love on the basis of performance.

Performance love falls short of God's love; His love would be no different from man's love if a person had to earn it. His is *agape* love and is desperately needed to give all kinds of love stature and a foundation. One translator describes it as "self-sacrificial love called out of the heart due to the preciousness of the object loved." God's children are His love objects—not because of what they are, but because of who He is!

Two ministers once stood praying by the bedside of little Sarah, a hideously burned two-year-old. Infection ravaged her body after the necessary skin grafts. After three cardiac arrests, the doctors wrote on her chart, "Death is imminent, parents notified." But, weary, dedicated nurses volunteered to stay on, and they worked feverishly through the night trying to save her life.

Although the doctors had said there was no hope, their love motivated their every effort. Sarah did live to be taken home in her mother's arms. It is similar with Christians. Though we were "disfigured" by sin and sentenced to die, God never gave up, and His love reached out to save and restore His children at any cost.

Longfellow wrote a poem on a worthless sheet of paper and it became worth $6,000. Rockefeller signed his name on scrap paper, and it was then worth millions. God in love writes His name on the sinner and transforms him into His precious child. "Behold, what manner of love the Father hath bestowed upon us, that we should be called the sons of God" (I John 3:1).

## Jesus Was Love Revealed

God was manifested in human flesh that we might see and understand His love. In a palace in Rome there is a high ceiling painted by one of the great masters, but it was beyond the range of vision, and its beauty obscure. Not wanting the masterpiece to remain unseen, the owner placed a highly polished mirror on the floor so that the picture could be seen in its reflection. Jesus came, "who is the image of the invisible God. . ." (Colossians 1:15), that all people could view His love and study His nature. Jesus, with "velvet steps" of love, crossed every boundary and barrier. He bewildered the religious leaders; His love was misunderstood, hated, rejected—and crucified.

## The Cross Was God at His Best and Man at His Worst

Love bore the sin that separated sinners from God (I Peter 2:24), and love reconciles them to God (Romans 5:10). Calvary conquered sin's dominion over the human race. There the penalty of every sin of spirit, soul, and body was paid.

The Cross is *proof* of God's love. Love gives, and God is a giver. "God so loved the world that he gave his only begotten Son, that whosoever believeth in him should not perish, but have everlasting life" (John 3:16). God created a body of flesh—a begotten Son—to dwell within to save humanity and to give them life.

Calvary was the complete embodiment of the kind of love described by Paul in his letter to the Corinthian church. (See I Corinthians 13:4-8.) At Calvary, love endured and was kind, was not jealous, did not display itself haughtily or in vain glory. It did not behave unbecomingly, was not conceited, arrogant, or rude.

Love did not insist on its own rights or its own way, for it was not self-seeking. It was not resentful, took no account of evil done to it as it suffered wrongly. Love did not rejoice in injustice and unrighteousness but only as truth and right prevailed. Love bore up under anything and everything that came, ready to believe the best in each of us— its hopes fadeless under all circumstances; it endured all things without weakening.

This was love at its zenith. The Cross cannot be viewed without its magnetic force drawing that person to love Christ. D. L. Moody once said, "I tell you there is one thing that draws above everything else in the world, and that is love." How powerful are the words of Jesus and so simply said, "And I, if I be lifted up from the earth, will draw all men unto me" (John 12:32).

When asked which was the first commandment, Jesus said, "And thou shalt love the Lord thy God with all thy heart, and with all thy soul, and with all thy mind, and with all thy strength: this is the first commandment" (Mark 12:30).

God wants our love; it is important to Him, for no one can love Him as His children can. Often people fear to express love because in doing so not only are their feelings revealed, but the revelation of their love makes them vulnerable to hurt by rejection. Christians can express their love to Him without fear of rejection—He loved us first, while we were yet unlovable. Another fear is that a person will be embarrassed if he expresses love because of established patterns of communication. God broke the pattern of sin's silence barrier, and as we draw nigh to God He responds by love and draws nigh to us!

Open communication maintains a closeness in relationships that would grow stagnant without the expression of love. Merely saying "I love you" as a forced action does not take much time but the nurturing of love needs time. The cultivating of love is an investment of a part of one's self. So, expressing love is not just vocalizing; it is the expression of a person's involvement in a relationship. If a person is out of touch with his feelings, it is virtually impossible to express them. When a Christian expresses his love to God, he is keeping in touch with his feelings about God and his involvement with Him. "Expressed" love has an important effect on the one who is expressing and "cementing" the relationship.

Eileen Gider wrote, "Love is the magic key of life, not to get what we want but to become what we ought to be."

Jesus encouraged Peter to express his feelings of love. Peter and the other disciples had been fishing in the Sea of Galilee during the night, and upon reaching shore they found Jesus and were invited to breakfast with Him. This led to Jesus' curious quizzing of Peter—asking three times about Peter's love for Him.

In response to each question of "Do you love Me?" Peter replied, "Lord, You know that I love You." After being asked the third time, he was grieved. Jesus gave him the opportunity to affirm *three* times what he had denied *three* times. Peter was encouraged to express His love, for he had a definite need to reaffirm verbally his love for Jesus. This gave him the opportunity to recommit himself to Christ and to service in His kingdom.

There is one never-failing source of love for every person. It is God, who is perfect love.

In their natural state, men fear to show and express love. This is because of man's imperfect, sinful nature which keeps him bound and unable to love, since sin is a state of rebellion against God. But because of His perfect nature, God could express perfectly His love by the redeeming act of the Cross, giving His life that men might have abundant life and be made free from the bondage of sin. This gives Christians freedom to love God and to express their love without fear!

Robin, a young married woman, was told by God in prayer, "Climb on My lap and let Me sit in the driver's seat." She related that as a little girl she loved to sit on her father's lap in the car and would remain there on long trips. God was preparing her for a traumatic journey ahead in her life. In the time of trial, she was secure in the assurance He was her loving Father and was "steering" her life.

Oh, what a blessed assurance there is in the fact God has chosen to portray His love in the role of a father to us, with His personal provision and protection! Christians are not mechanical robots, but as His children they can "climb on His lap," let Him be in the driver's seat, tell Him how much they love and trust Him, and let Him direct their lives.

## Love Is a Commitment

It is not an emotional roller coaster but it involves both rights and responsibilities. Jesus instructed, "If ye love me, keep my commandments" (John 14:15).

When a person loves Jesus, obedience is not a grievous duty or dreary obligation. Paul declared, "For the love of Christ controls, and urges and impels us" (II Corinthians 5:14, *The Amplified Bible*).

After loving God, the second commandment is "Thou shalt love thy neighbour as thyself. There is none other commandment greater than these" (Mark 12:31).

The second commandment is impossible without obeying the first, for as much as a person loves God, in the same degree he is capable of loving others. The fruit of the Spirit in Galatians 5:22-23, is love, joy, peace, longsuffering, gentleness, goodness, faith, meekness, and temperance: against such there is no law, for His nature is the "complete garment" that we wear. "Love worketh no ill to his neighbour: therefore love is the fulfilling of the law" (Romans 13:10), and this is the intended way of life.

Jesus did not say to love your neighbor and hate yourself. (See Galatians 5:14; Romans 13:9.) The requirement to love yourself is given with the command to love your neighbor. When a person realizes that God loves him and accepts him, only then is he able to accept himself with his limitations and weaknesses! Self-acceptance causes a person to cease revolving about "self," always selfishly seeking acceptance, and frees him to turn selflessly outward to others and love his neighbor.

Dag Hammerskjold put it this way: "He who is at war with himself is at war with others."

## Loving God and Loving Others

"We love him, because he first loved us" (I John 4:19).

A Christian's love for God will burst forth in love for others. Loving others is a test of a person's own love for God. (See I John 4:8, 21.)

This love for others is the proof of genuine salvation! (I John 3:14). Someone has said that the greatest factor that limits the church is "man's inhumanity to man." Christians are admonished to "not love in word, neither in tongue; but in deed and in truth" (I John 3:18).

Love is demonstrated by people's behavior in relation to others. Jesus said, "By this shall all men know that ye are my disciples, if ye have love one to another" (John 13:35).

Psychologists call this current age "the Age of Human Relations" because people getting along with each other is such an overwhelming problem. There is no way human love alone can cope with the pressures of everyday living in this abrasive twentieth century! Christians need the dynamic power of His love to practice His divine dimension of living.

The Early Church was remarkably, decisively, and distinctly different from others in the world. "They took knowledge of them, that they had been with Jesus" (Acts 4:13). They were filled with Jesus' love and this power in them caused an explosion in the Roman Empire.

Jesus said there would be a "fountain within!" "He who believes in Me—who cleaves to and trusts in and relies on Me—as the Scripture has said, Out from his innermost being springs and rivers of living water shall flow (continuously)" (John 7:38, *The Amplified Bible*). He was speaking of the Spirit that would be given. His nature of love is like an artesian well springing up, splashing over, overflowing, engulfing and flowing out to the world—curing hate, solving life's problems, pulverizing prejudices, oiling life's frictions, and healing the soul, body and mind.

In writing to the church at Philippi, Paul urged "that your love may abound yet more and more" (Philippians 1:9). A Christian's love is to abound like waves rolling in and overflowing in every direction. They are not to be as the Dead Sea, having an inlet but no outlet—always receiving but never giving! Just as the muscles of the body become flabby and the whole physical system loses its tone without exercise, the Christian's spiritual life will lose strength unless he exercises love by giving out to others.

## Expressions of His Love to a Lost World

It was love that brought Jesus "to seek and to save that which was lost" (Luke 19:10).

Love and labor are inseparable; love shows itself by action through service! Love is the giving of time and energy in witnessing and discipling. It is willing to be involved in the hurt and the pain of others. Love that God has placed in the hearts of His children reaches out to those who are lost and dying in the loveless desert of this world.

These are days the Bible said would lack love and it would be one of the signs of the endtime. Jesus said that the love of many would wax cold (Matthew 24:12). One writer wrote that perilous times would come and men would be lovers of their own selves, and lovers of pleasure more than lovers of God (II Timothy 3:1, 4).

It is in this hour that Christians are encouraged to "Keep yourselves in the love of God, looking for the mercy of our Lord Jesus Christ unto eternal life" (Jude 21). His love has plans for His children that will continue throughout eternity. His call of love will say, "Rise up, my love," and Christians will be changed in a moment, in the twinkling of an eye to meet the Lord in the air and so shall we ever be with the Lord (I Thessalonians 4:17).

## Test Your Knowledge

### True or False

_____ 1. Love is the answer to many physical and mental disorders.

_____ 2. The disease, marasmus, is caused by a lack of food and care.

_____ 3. Material things help to fulfill the basic human need for love.

_____ 4. Nothing can separate us from the love of God.

_____ 5. There are at least three Greek words which describe various relationships of love.

_____ 6. *Agape* love is the supreme love such as that manifested by God toward us.

_____ 7. Jesus Christ was love revealed.

_____ 8. There is really no physical proof of God's love.

_____ 9. Love shows itself by action through service.

_____10. One way we love God is by loving others.

## Apply Your Knowledge

Realizing the power of love to lift up and edify, it would be good if Christians would express their love more—to parents, children, friends, and fellow Christians. The world would be blessed greatly by a concerted effort by all people to show their love for one another.

Why not sit down and write those long overdue letters? There is a definite power in written words of love and appreciation. You could be a blessing to someone special by only taking a few minutes to write.

Another possibility would be making some unexpected phone calls. You may be surprised how it can lift others' spirits and cheer them to hear from you. To know you care is the most important message they can receive.

## Expand Your Knowledge

Love is one of the basic needs of humanity, and the lack of it can cause depression such as is covered in the following chapter. Take time to study and meditate on the Scriptures for chapter five.

# Survival Kit
# for the Depressed

*These things I have spoken unto you, that in me ye might have peace. In the world ye shall have tribulation: but be of good cheer; I have overcome the world.*

*John 16:33*

---

**Start With the Scriptures**

I Kings 17; 18; 19:1-8  Ephesians 4:26-27
Romans 12:17-21  Philippians 4:4-11

---

Alice awakened groggily at the ringing of the 6:15 a.m. alarm. As the fogginess lifted, she was aware of an uneasiness that enveloped her. What was wrong? Then she remembered. Yesterday her supervisor had informed her that due to the poor economy, the company had to cut back. She was given a month's notice.

Alice had worked with the company for only a year, taking the job after her husband's death. Ron...Ron! She still missed him. The feelings of loss and grief returned, adding to her misery. She knew she must find another job to support her two children, but she felt that she did not have enough energy even to get out of bed. Unbidden, tears began coursing down her cheeks as she sobbed uncontrollably.

Is there hope for Alice—and the millions suffering from depression? In his book, *How To Win Over Depression,* Tim LaHaye calls depression the number one emotional illness in America. Crisis hotlines in major cities receive suicide calls daily.

The term *depression* is commonly used in speaking of a gamut of symptoms—from "the blues" to disturbed thinking patterns and suicidal thoughts. Other symptoms are pessimism, feelings of gloom, helplessness, despondency, dejection, hopelessness, a tendency to cry, irritability, hostility, anxiety, loss of interest or concentration, social withdrawal, changes in eating habits, disturbed sleep patterns, and energy loss.

Depression is no respecter of social standing or of age. Neither the wealthy nor the famous are immune to its attacks. President Abraham Lincoln and England's Queen Elizabeth I reportedly suffered from depression.

Everyone at some point in his life will probably have some symptoms of depression. The duration of the symptoms determine its severity. Minor depression may last a few days or a few months but usually disappears with time. Continual depression may be a symptom of psychiatric or physical illness.

To answer the question posed previously, yes, there is hope for Alice—and for anyone who is depressed.

Before considering some specific ways to deal with depression, let us look at its causes. In some instances, such as the death of a loved one, the cause is obvious. However, man is such a complex being that often depression cannot be traced to one specific factor. The spiritual, emotional, and physical parts of man are so intertwined that they are inseparable. Therefore, a problem in one area usually affects the other areas as well. However, for ease of discussion, we will consider these three areas separately.

## Spiritual

Sin and its resultant guilt causes depression. The only remedy is to confess sin and receive forgiveness for it.

A person who has never come to God in repentance carries a tremendous load of guilt for a lifetime of sinful deeds. When he realizes that he is a sinner and follows the biblical steps of repentance, baptism in the name of Jesus Christ for the remission of sins, and receiving the promised Holy Spirit, he feels like and is a new person. (See Acts 2:38; II Corinthians 5:17.) His depression is gone!

During the course of life, however, the euphoria of this new experience may fade. The Christian may neglect to schedule a personal time of prayer and meditating on the Word. He may get caught up in trying to solve problems on his own without seeking the help of God. Being yet an imperfect human being, he makes mistakes. He may do things without thinking, which he later realizes were wrong. When guilt overcomes him, it brings along its companion—depression. The solution, again, is repentance: "If we confess our sins, he is faithful and just to forgive us our sins, and to cleanse us from all unrighteousness" (I John 1:9).

Sometimes, it is easier for God to forgive us than it is for us to forgive ourselves. After God has forgiven us, we should follow the example of Apostle Paul: "Forgetting those things which are behind, and reaching forth unto those things which are before, I press toward the mark for the prize of the high calling of God in Christ Jesus" (Philippians 3:13-14).

## Physical

Many scientists believe that depression can be caused by a chemical imbalance in the brain, although some admit that they do not know whether the mind thinking depressed thoughts causes the biochemical changes or whether the chemical imbalance in the brain causes the depression.

Of special note are the thyroid and adrenal glands. A *Reader's Digest* article from the December, 1983, issue suggests a simple home test for low thyroid or low adrenal function (Heilman, p. 95-96). A doctor can do a more thorough check.

Depression is also one symptom of hypoglycemia (low blood sugar) which can be controlled by diet. A physician can prescribe a five-hour glucose tolerance test to determine if hypoglycemia is a problem. The recommended diet avoids refined sugar, white flour, and caffeine. Five or six small meals, high in protein and low in carbohydrates, are recommended to keep the blood sugar on a more even level. Even people who do not test as hypoglycemic often benefit from the hypoglycemia diet.

Depression is a side effect of some medications. The *Reader's Digest* article cited above states, "According to the National Institute of Mental Health, oral contraceptives, barbiturates, steroids such as cortisone, some antibiotics such as the sulfonamides, and some drugs used to control hypertension, such as reserpine, can trigger depression" (Heilman, p. 96). One should ask his doctor or pharmacist about possible side effects of prescribed medication or check the *Physician's Desk Reference,* available in the local public library.

Perhaps women are more prone to depression than men because of their biological differences. Postpartum depression following childbirth is common. As was mentioned earlier, depression may be a side effect of oral contraceptives. Many women find themselves regularly battling PMS (premenstrual syndrome), with depression being one of the factors. Depression may also affect women during menopause.

## Emotional

Depression can be caused by many emotional factors.

*Loss.* A permanent loss such as the death of a loved one or the loss of a limb due to accident or amputation because of disease can be traumatic.

Even a temporary loss, such as losing one's job or health, can lead to depression. If a person has had a long bout with illness, he may feel as if he will never regain his health. In addition to depression being a symptom of some diseases, the patient's mental attitude of hopelessness may add to his despair.

As strange as it may seem, reaching one's goal represents a type of loss. Having a goal gives a person something to reach for, to work toward. Once it has been achieved, the goal is no longer there. The joy of achievement may soon be followed by depression unless the person has wisely set a new goal for himself.

*Disappointment.* Failing to get an expected promotion, failing an employment test, having to postpone a long-awaited vacation, or not getting the loan for which one has applied are only a few examples of many disappointments that could be listed. Although one should expect the best, having an alternative may prevent depression due to disappointment.

*Pressure.* Everyone faces pressures in all stages of life. Some pressure is good. For example, a change in jobs can be positive, yet pressure can result in relocating, facing new responsibilities, learning new job tasks, and making new friends.

However, if a person is losing control in a pressure situation, feels trapped by his circumstances, or can see no hope for future relief, the pressure becomes a negative force, resulting in unhealthy stress and depression. Properly managing pressure by maintaining a good mental attitude will prevent the depression associated with pressure.

*Anger.* Some authorities believe that anger is a consideration in every case of depression. Consciously or subconsciously, one may be angry with the person responsible for his loss or disappointment. He may be angry with God for allowing it to happen or with himself for not doing more to prevent its occurrence. Anger improperly dealt with becomes repressed anger, leading to depression. To be freed from such depression, the person must first deal with the anger.

*Low self-esteem.* Perhaps one of the greatest causes of depression is the lack of self-acceptance. In his book, *How To Win Over Depression,* Tim LaHaye states that every depressed person he has ever counseled has had a problem with self-acceptance. Another counselor, Dr. James Dobson, states in his book, *Dr. Dobson Answers Your Questions,* "Lack of self-esteem produces more symptoms of psychiatric disorders than any other factor yet identified." In another passage he states, "More than any other factor, it is the root cause of depression." If this be true, developing a positive self-image is necessary to overcoming depression. (See Chapter One for a more detailed discussion of self-esteem.)

*Self-pity.* Elijah succumbed to self-pity, the details of which are recorded in the nineteenth chapter of I Kings. Only a short time after his tremendous victory over the prophets of Baal, he became so depressed he wanted to die. He said, "It is enough; now, O LORD, take away my life" (I Kings 19:4). One reason for his depression was that he allowed self-pity to invade his mind. He felt all alone: "I, even I only, am left" (I Kings 19:10).

Self-pity can come through an unwillingness to accept present circumstances. Although the Apostle Paul had many trying times, he was not depressed, for he said, "We are troubled on every side, yet not distressed; we are perplexed, but not in despair; Persecuted, but not forsaken; cast down, but not destroyed" (II Corinthians 4:8-9). His secret was trusting God in every circumstance: "For I have learned, in whatsoever state I am, therewith to be content" (Philippians 4:11).

## Aids to Survival

Remember Job? He lost all his children, his possessions, and his health. His wife and friends gave him no encouragement. His depression was apparent in this statement: "Let the day perish wherein I was born" (Job 3:3). Yet, even when he felt that God had deserted him, he proclaimed, "But he knoweth the way that I take: when he hath tried me, I shall come forth as gold" (Job 23:10). Job did indeed come forth. The final chapter records that "the LORD gave Job twice as much as he had before" (Job 42:10).

You, too, can come victoriously through the valley of depression. Twelve suggestions are given here to help you.

1. *Face the situation.* Examine your feelings and try to identify the factor that triggered your depres-

sion. If the problem can be remedied, set goals and take steps to reach them. For example, if being overweight is causing you to be depressed, set a weight-loss goal and go on a diet.

If the situation triggering your depression cannot be changed, accept it. The well-known "Serenity Prayer" states: "God, grant me the serenity to accept the things I cannot change, the courage to change the things I can, and the wisdom to know the difference."

You may need to ask God to help you accept the situation. You may not want to face the fact that a loved one is gone, that a leg has been amputated, that your children are marrying and leaving home, or that you are getting older. Yet, if emotional healing is to come, you must face reality.

2. *Talk with someone about your problem, but do not broadcast it.* Sharing the problem with another makes the burden much lighter, but sharing it with too many may prove to be detrimental. Long after you have victoriously overcome, some people may be unwilling to forget, holding the past against you unjustly.

Therefore, choose your confidant with care. A close friend who can keep a confidence, a minister, or someone who has successfully overcome similar difficulties can provide helpful insight.

Besides clarifying the problem in your own mind, in talking with someone you will often discover a solution you had not thought of previously. The person may also be able to help with a solution to the problem. For instance, if you need a job, he may know of a suitable one.

3. *Schedule a time of personal devotion.* Choose a consistent method of Bible study rather than opening the Bible at random and reading a verse. Such an approach is not the best way to fight depression. A systematic study of the Bible with an emphasis

on help for the particular problem at hand is much more effective.

Effective prayer is an important part of personal devotion. But a whining, complaining "prayer" focusing on how terrible your problem is and how bad you feel, perhaps even accusing God of being unfair, will only foster self-pity. A person who prays in such a manner is actually comitting sin because he is putting himself above God, in effect saying that he knows better than God what is best for him. We should follow the Apostle Paul's admonition: "Be careful for nothing; but in every thing by prayer and supplication with thanksgiving let your requests be made known unto God. And the peace of God, which passeth all understanding, shall keep your hearts and minds through Christ Jesus" (Philippians 4:6-7).

4. *Maintain a spirit of thanksgiving.* "In every thing give thanks: for this is the will of God in Christ Jesus concerning you" (I Thessalonians 5:18). Even in the most difficult situation, one can find something for which to thank God. Even in her sorrow, a widow can be thankful for the years she shared with her husband, for his provision for her, for their children and for the happy times.

Although you cannot always see it at the time, the Bible promises that "all things work together for good to them that love God, to them who are the called according to his purpose" (Romans 8:28).

5. *Memorize Scripture.* Saturate your mind with Scriptures of promise. Carrying small cards with Scriptures printed on them can provide meaningful activity during odd moments throughout the day—waiting at stop lights or standing in line—and help to keep your mind off your depression.

6. *Upgrade your vocabulary.* If you have found yourself making statements like "I just can't make it through this" or "It's a hopeless situation," determine now to eliminate such statements from your

vocabulary. Replace them with positive statements such as "I can do all things through Christ which strengtheneth me" (Philippians 4:13).

7. *Read.* The Bible should come first, of course, but other good literature is also helpful. As Emily Dickinson wrote, "There is no frigate like a book to take us lands away." A good book can transport its reader into another country or another century, and when he mentally returns to the present, he may find that he can view the situation more objectively.

8. *Listen to music.* In the Old Testament, King Saul found that his troubled mind was soothed by David's playing on his harp. The right kind of music still has the same effect. Choose your music carefully. If you have a good Christian radio station in your area, tune it in. Otherwise, listen to spirit-lifting music on records and tapes.

9. *Keep busy.* Physical activity seems to aid good emotional health. Do something creative—tend your garden, remodel a room, make new curtains, cook, work at a hobby—anything that will keep your mind productively occupied. Enroll in a class you have always wanted to take. Volunteer to help in a nursing home, hospital, or community service organization. Become more involved in church activities. Reaching out to others is an effective antidote to depression.

10. *Stay socially active.* Although you may feel like withdrawing from society, make a special effort to socialize. By all means, attend church regularly. Some people make the mistake of skipping church when they are depressed, thus denying themselves a valuable means of overcoming depression.

If you are invited to someone's home for an evening, go, even if you do not really want to. If you are sitting at home feeling lonely, invite someone over. Research has shown that people who maintain their personal relationships, especially in times of crises or changes in their lives, are more likely to come through in good mental health than those who try to make it on their own.

11. *Take care of your body.* Stress and depression can take a toll on the body's resources. In addition, loss of appetite is one symptom of depression. However, in addition to depriving a person of essential nutrients, not eating well may lead to physical complications such as an ulcer. Eating more frequently may help. Also one might consider taking vitamins, especially vitamins C and B-complex which are sometimes called the "stress vitamins."

However, vitamins should not be taken indiscriminately. Some can be toxic. For example, too much vitamin A or D can be harmful. Also, a person who wishes to take vitamin E should build up the amount gradually. People with high blood pressure or a rheumatic heart condition should be especially careful, as there is some indication that too much vitamin E can aggravate these conditions. Many books are on the market today which describe the various vitamins and their uses.

Since the depressed person may feel apathetic, it may be difficult for him to get motivated. Exercising with a friend may help. Exercise gives one a feeling of accomplishment and lessens the sense of helplessness.

The depressed person should attempt to get enough sleep to refresh the body, but he should not use sleep as an escape mechanism. Sleeping during the day may lead to insomnia at night. If a person has trouble sleeping because of depression, he should quote Scripture passages or think of pleasant thoughts rather than dwelling on his depression.

12. *Create a "spirit lifter" file.* David, who wrote many psalms of encouragement, also encountered depression. In one psalm, he wrote, "Why art thou cast down, O my soul?" (Psalm 42:5). Yet, "David

encouraged himself in the LORD his God" (I Samuel 30:6). One way to encourage yourself is to create a "spirit lifter" file.

You do not need to wait until you are depressed to begin this project. In a folder or manila envelope, keep items that are special to you. You might include cards and notes of appreciation from friends or people you have helped in the past, favorite verses of Scripture, and uplifting pamphlets or articles. Include your written testimonies of how God has brought you through trials in the past. Whenever you begin to feel depressed, a look through this special personal file should help to encourage you.

Although it is possible, depression does not often vanish overnight. The passing of time helps, but you can actively work to bring about quicker recovery by following the above suggestions.

Present circumstances will not last forever. They will change. You *can* make it. Just keep holding on. When you have come victoriously through the valley of depression, you can look back in triumph and see how the hand of God was guiding thorughout the journey. "Lo, I am with you alway, even unto the end of the world" (Matthew 28:20).

## Test Your Knowledge

1. Depression has been labeled by some as the number one _____ illness in America.

2. List three of the many symptoms of depression: _____, _____, and _____.

3. Depression can affect the _____, _____, or _____ part of a person.

4. _____ is the cause for spiritual depression.

5. Many scientists believe depression can be caused by a _____ imbalance in the brain.

6. _____ is a physical disorder that often produces depression as one of its symptoms.

7. Maintaining a good _____ will help manage pressure and prevent depression associated with it.

8. Unwillingness to accept present circumstances can create _____.

9. In overcoming depression one must first _____ the situation.

10. A major key in overcoming depression is staying socially _____.

## Apply Your Knowledge

Follow the advice given under suggestion number twelve by creating a "spirit lifter" file. The time to begin collecting cards and edifying notes or letters is while you are not depressed. You will not want to start such a collection when you are depressed. A good collection of encouraging items can assist you in warding off an onslaught of depression.

Even if you never experience depression, it is very edifying to look through subtle reminders of past good times and friends for it can cheer you in the present time.

## Expand Your Knowledge

The next chapter is on the gifts of the Spirit and their proper use. Read the Scriptures for the chapter before continuing that you may have a good foundation of Bible background. You may also want to be especially alert to the operation of the gifts in your church. These things will prepare you for the study of this vital chapter.

# Gifts that Edify

*How is it then, brethren? when ye come together, every one of you hath a psalm, hath a doctrine, hath a tongue, hath a revelation, hath an interpretation. Let all things be done unto edifying.*

*I Corinthians 14:26*

### Start With the Scriptures

Romans 12:6-8; 14:19; 15:2
I Corinthians 12; 14
I Thessalonians 5:11

The minister was well into his message when there was a sudden outburst of prophecy from the back of the congregation. The confusion in the audience was immediate. What was happening here? Was not God already speaking to the people through the minister? Why was this additional message needed at this time? Which message should give way to the other?

The pastor acted quickly to allay the confusion by asking the person who had interrupted to be seated until after the message was concluded. In obedience, this very sincere person sat down somewhat confused. But the confusion in the church subsided and the service progressed. After the service, the pastor wisely took the one who had spoken into his office for some instruction on how the gifts of the Spirit operate in the body of Christ.

## Proper Concept of the Church Body

It is extremely important when considering the operation of the gifts of the Spirit that there is a proper understanding of the structure, function, and authority of the church. If a person does not have a proper concept of the church, then he certainly will not properly value things pertaining to the church. If he does not understand the Bride, then he will not understand the gifts that were given to the Bride.

It is obvious from reading the Corinthian letters that the people had a problem with their concept of the church. The Corinthians' divisions and party spirits did not foster fellowship but, rather, fractured it. Paul warned them with these words: "Ye come together not for the better, but for the worse" (I Corinthians 11:17). It would have been more profitable for them not to be together, in this instance, because of their attitude toward one another. Instead of leaving the meetings built up and encouraged, they departed confused and down in spirit.

The members at Corinth did not realize their divisions were a result of their wrong concept of the church—the body of Christ. Paul tried to show them that he, Peter, and Apollos were different ministers sent to the church for the same purpose—the upbuilding of the body of Christ. (See I Corinthians 3:5-9.)

Not only did the Corinthians fail to respect the ministries that God gave them, but they did not hold a high appreciation for other members of the body of Christ. That is why Paul addressed them concerning their conduct at the communion table. (See I Corinthians 11.) In verse 28 of that chapter, the apostle told them that a person should have a time of self-examination before approaching the Lord's supper; otherwise, he eats and drinks damnation to himself. He said that some had become sick and others had fallen asleep, possibly a reference to death, because of a wrong approach to the communion. (See I Corinthians 11:30.)

The key phrase to Paul's instructions was, "Not discerning the Lord's body" (I Corinthians 11:29). They apparently did not have a proper appreciation for His body. Which body? The one that hung on the cross? Partially. But Paul's main emphasis in I Corinthians was the coordination and unity of Christ's body on earth—the church.

Even though people are saved as individuals, they find their spiritual health and longevity in the body of Christ. The gifts of healing were given by the Bridegroom, Jesus Christ, to His bride, the church. By failing to celebrate the communion properly, many Christians did not receive the benefits given to the body of Christ.

## Unity in the Body

When Jesus took the loaf, broke it, and gave it to the disciples, it represented two things. The loaf represented His physical body and certainly should have told them that the one sacrifice would be offered to them all. When they ate it, they were accepting the fact that whatever their talents, ambitions, or backgrounds, it took the same sacrifice for them all. This common denominator should have helped bring them together.

Secondly, the loaf represented the unity of the

church He was establishing and for whom His body was being broken. It was not biscuits or cookies, but one single loaf. When they broke off a piece of the bread, they should have realized that as individuals they were part of the whole body, connected to each other by the common atonement of Christ.

Instructions concerning the gifts of the Spirit were given in the context of the unity of the body. That was the central theme of Paul's instructions to the church. The ministry is given to unite the body; the Lord's supper should serve to bring people together; and the gifts of the Spirit are given for the unity and edification of the church.

## Bride Endowed with Gifts

*God gave His bride the gift of leadership.* God gave to the church apostles, prophets, evangelists, pastors, and teachers. (See Ephesians 4:11 and I Corinthians 12:28.) These are individuals God calls to minister to and feed His children and to bring them to maturity.

These ministers and their ministries serve like the nerve system from the head of the body to the feet. There are five major categories of nerves in the human body, and there are five categories of ministry that relay the will of the Head of the body, which is Christ, to the diverse members of the church.

*God gives gifts of the Spirit.* These are more than anointed talents or the natural abilities of leaders yielded to the Spirit. These gifts operate under the leadership of the ministry but are not confined to the ministry. Many Christian laymen have been mightily used of the Lord in the various gifts of the Spirit.

The gifts of the Spirit should not be confused with the fruit of the Spirit as described in Galatians 5:22, which should be evident in every Spirit-filled child of God. The gifts of the Spirit should operate, however, under the influence of the fruit of the Spirit.

These gifts of the Spirit are channels of communication and ministry that do not originate in human thinking but come directly from the Spirit of God. They do flow through human personalities that are yielded to the Spirit, but they are supernatural.

The church must have the gifts of the Spirit operable because they are the rightful inheritance of God's people. God intended for His church to possess them. It should be noted that even though there was a misuse of the gifts in the Corinthian congregation, Paul did not attempt to stop the operation of these ministries. He said he did not want them to come behind in any gift (I Corinthians 1:7). He concluded chapter 14 by saying, "Forbid not to speak with tongues." He only wanted to bring balance, regulation, control, and edification to the church. The Holy Spirit was not out of control. It was the people, the human vessels through which the Spirit flows, that were undisciplined.

## Purpose of the Gifts of the Spirit

There are three basic reasons why God gave the gifts of the Spirit to the church. *First, they were given for the edification, upbuilding, and unifying of the body.* The word *edify* implies a charging up, like a weak battery on a car receiving more power by being connected to another power source. Likewise, the church is "charged up" by the proper operation of the gifts of the Spirit. The numerous exhortations to the church to edify one another should be practiced by all Christians. "Seek that ye may excel to the edifying of the church" (I Corinthians 14:12).

*The second reason the gifts are given to the church is for a supernatural identity.* Paul said that unbelievers in the service would not be repelled by the move of the Spirit. (See I Corinthians 14:24-25.) On the contrary, when they see the beautiful harmony and flow of the Spirit among the various members of the body, they will acknowledge that God is in the midst of His people.

*The third reason for the gifts is that the church faces a monumental task of carrying out the great commission to preach the gospel to every creature.* To meet this challenge, the church needs the supernatural gifts of the Spirit to energize it. The Spirit works with the church in accomplishing the task. As long as the church faces the task of world evangelism, there will always be a need for the gifts of the Spirit.

## Categories of the Gifts

The twelfth chapter of I Corinthians lists nine gifts of the Spirit in verses 8-10. These nine can be categorized in three sets of three. These are the *gifts of utterance* (prophecy, divers kinds of tongues, interpretation of tongues), *gifts of revelation* (word of wisdom, word of knowledge, discerning of spirits), and the *gifts of power* (faith, working of miracles, gifts of healing). Although there may be other gifts mentioned elsewhere in Scripture, only those listed in this Scripture setting will be dealt with at this time.

## Gifts of Utterance

*Prophecy is the Spirit imparting a supernatural message which an individual gives to the church in his native tongue.* There is no "unknown tongue speaking" involved in this gift, hence there is no need for interpretation. Certainly prophecy could be included in the preaching ministry, but it is not limited to preaching. It is a message of direction or comfort given by God through a yielded vessel to the church. Paul gave specific guidelines for prophecy (I Corinthians 14:29-33).

There is to be a limit of two or three prophecies. This eliminated a constant series of proclamations. Paul wrote that the people should not interrupt one another but allow one to speak at a time to avoid confusion. He gave the leadership and congregation the right to judge the prophecy. Not everything that comes under the guise of the Spirit is of God. The spirit of the prophet is subject to the prophet. He can control his actions and thus has no excuse for irresponsible utterances.

*There are six purposes for speaking in tongues listed in the Scripture:*
- Evidence of the baptism of the Holy Ghost (Acts 2:4)
- Speaking supernaturally to God (Romans 8:26-27; I Corinthians 14:2)
- Magnifying God (Acts 2:11)
- Edifying or building up oneself (I Corinthians 14:4; Jude 20)
- Sign to the unbeliever (I Corinthians 14:22)
- A message to the church that needs an interpreter (I Corinthians 14:27-28).

Paul declared that he spoke in tongues devotionally. In fact, he said, "I thank my God, I speak with tongues more than ye all" (I Corinthians 14:18). Earlier in the chapter he validated devotional tongues as communication with God where the Spirit prays and the mind is at rest.

*Most of I Corinthians 14 deals with the need for an interpretation of a message given to the church in a tongue unknown to the congregation.* Unless there is an interpretation of such a message, the people will not be blessed. Visitors may think the people are mentally unbalanced if no one reveals what was said. The Apostle Paul said that even though he prayed in tongues more than any of them, he would rather speak five words in a language the church understood because he wanted the people to be blessed by the Spirit (I Corinthians 14:19). In verses 27 and 28, he established similar guidelines for tongues as he did for prophecy. If there is no interpretation of the message in tongues, the speaker should pray that he himself may interpret (verse 13) or else keep quiet (verse 28) and pray devotionally.

## Gifts of Revelation

*The word of wisdom is divine direction given by the Spirit of God during a time of difficulty or decision.* This word will not come about as a part of the normal reasoning process but will suddenly drop into the mind of a yielded, sensitive person. It is more than a human word that is fitly spoken. It is the divine word at the right moment.

*The word of knowledge is giving forth facts that are known only to God.* An example of how this gift can function was shown when a pastor and some of his elders went to the hospital to pray for a woman who had been ill. As they prayed, the Spirit of the Lord suddenly came upon one of the elders and gave him insight into what was in the woman's mind. By the Spirit's prompting, he told her the secrets of her heart. She was feigning illness to retaliate against her family. The Spirit spoke to her through this elder to spare her the impending heartaches that would result if she carried her scheme to completion.

*The discerning of spirits is an insight God gives His people, particularly leaders, into the spirit world regarding motives.* It is God's gift to keep the church from being deceived by seducing spirits. The Apostle John referred to this gift when he said, "Beloved, believe not every spirit, but try the spirits whether they are of God: because many false prophets are gone out into the world" (I John 4:1).

Not everyone who declares, "Thus saith the Lord" is of God. It is necessary for motives to be tested, and the Holy Spirit is a discerner, along with the Word of God (Hebrews 4:12).

## Gifts of Power

*The gifts of power include the gift of faith.* There is a difference between this gift of faith and the faith that every man needs to please the Lord. A person cannot come to God without faith (Hebrews 11:6). God has given every man a measure of faith (Romans 12:3). Everyone has a certain amount of faith, but the gift of faith given to the church is a supernatural confidence to believe God in an hour of need. It could be during an hour of despair, sickness, national calamity, church trouble, or family problems. Paul exercised this gift when he stood on the deck of the storm-tossed ship and encouraged everyone on board that there would be no loss of life. (See Acts 27:21-25.)

*The gifts of miracles and healing work in conjunction with the gift of faith but are not limited to it.* The working of miracles is the altering of the very course of nature to such an extent that it cannot be attributed to man's ability or to circumstances, but only to God. God will endow some Christian with His power to work a miracle that will arrest the attention of men and focus their minds on the all-powerful God. Whereas gifts of healing deal with the body, the gift of miracles works in the area of circumstances and even nature.

A number of witnesses have told of a time when

a rural area had been without rain for so long that the region faced certain disaster. Even though no rain was in the forecast, the church began to pray, and rain fell only in that area. Meteorologists could not explain the sudden appearance of rain, but the church gave thanks to God.

*The gifts of healing are for the repairing and restoring of mental and physical health.* These gifts were abundantly evident in the Early Church but certainly were not limited to that era. Healing is in the atonement of Jesus Christ and is part of the inheritance of God's children. God has used and will continue to use certain individuals to minister healing to His people. These people have been ministers and laymen alike. Christians are instructed to call for the elders to anoint them and pray the prayer of faith over them (James 5:14). There have been numerous occasions where a member of the body of Christ was used to minister healing to another.

The gifts of healing have been some of the greatest tools God has used for the advancement of the gospel. Many people around the turn of the century came to God because of miracles of healing that God performed in their lives.

## Love Is the Key

A study of the gifts would not be complete without emphasizing that between the two chapters given to the discussion of the gifts lies I Corinthians 13, the beautiful chapter describing love. It is no accident that the love chapter is located there because the gifts of the Spirit must always operate in the love of God. Love is the bottom line of Christianity. If one could speak with the tongues of men and of angels and did not have love, he would profit nothing.

The nine gifts of the Spirit listed in I Corinthians 12 must work harmoniously with the nine attributes of the fruit of the Spirit in Galatians 5:22, and be characterized by the nine descriptions of love listed in I Corinthians 13. Love is described as kind, patient, generous, humble, courteous, unselfish, good tempered, without guile, and sincere. In order for the Spirit to function properly, each member of the body of Christ must minister in love.

In learning to move in step and harmony with the Spirit, members of the body will make some mistakes. We sometimes forget that even with the best intentions and the most sincere motives, Christians are human and can miss the intent of the voice of the Spirit.

That happened in the Early Church. Agabus, a prophet, was used in the gift of prophecy concerning the Apostle Paul. After he spoke, the people begged Paul not to go to Jerusalem. The Spirit did not tell Paul to stay out of Jerusalem, but that he would be bound there. Paul knew that would happen and had consecrated himself to that possibility. Paul did not miss the will of God by going into Jerusalem, but it is possible that some of the people misunderstood what the Spirit was saying.

If a person makes a mistake in the exercise of the gifts, he should submit to God's anointed leadership in the church for instruction. A mistake should not hinder that person from further ministry. He should continue to learn how to flow with the Spirit so he can be used to communicate clearly the will of God to the church.

## Test Your Knowledge

1. If one is to understand the gifts of the Spirit, it is essential to have a proper concept of the _____.

2. The _____ church had a definite problem with this concept.

3. Their many _____ were caused by their wrong concept of the church body.

4. There are _____ categories of ministry that relay God's will to the diverse membership of the church.

5. The gifts of the Spirit are given for the edifying, upbuilding, and _____ of the body of Christ.

6. There are three basic categories of the gifts of the Spirit: _____, _____, and _____.

7. Paul said, "I thank my God, I speak with _____ more than ye all."

8. The gifts of power include the gift of faith, gifts of miracles, and gifts of _____.

9. The gifts of the Spirit must always operate in the _____ of God.

10. Love is the key to proper _____ of the gifts.

## Apply Your Knowledge

Apostle Paul said, "Covet earnestly the best gifts." It is good to be used by the Holy Spirit for the edification of Christ's body.

There is nothing wrong with seeking to be used in the operation of the gifts as long as your motive is right. If you are not used greatly in the gifts, try making yourself more available to God to be used for His glory. God is seeking for those who will be sensitive in yielding to His Spirit.

## Expand Your Knowledge

For a further examination of one of God's gifts to the church, read on to chapter seven, "The Ministry—God's Gift to the Church." Study the preparatory Scriptures before reading the chapter.

# The Ministry—
# God's Gift
# to the Church

*And he gave some, apostles; and some, prophets; and some, evangelists; and some, pastors and teachers; For the perfecting of the saints, for the work of the ministry, for the edifying of the body of Christ.*

*Ephesians 4:11-12*

---

### Start With the Scriptures

Matthew 28:18-20  
Romans 10:15-17  
I Corinthians 1:18-21; 4:9-15  
Hebrews 5:11-14

---

It seemed that their prayers had been in vain. Where was their God? Had He forgotten their plight in the land of bondage? And if He had heard their cries, what was He waiting for?

God had indeed heard the pleas of the Children of Israel. Not one of their tears had gone unnoticed; but if God had heard their prayers over a period of several years in the land of Egypt, why had He not responded sooner? Why was He delaying His answer?

What seemed to be a delay in God's answering the prayers of Israel was actually the time that was necessary to prepare a man to lead the people out of their bondage and govern them.

## God's Form of Government

God's method of government for Israel is called a *theocracy,* which means, "God rule." It is the ability for God to rule His people through the channel of an anointed leader. God was developing the leader who would be instrumental in delivering Israel out of Egypt. His name was Moses.

Exodus 3 relates the story of Moses' call to leadership. God told Moses that He had empathized with the need of the people: "I have surely seen the affliction of my people. . .and have heard their cry by reason of their taskmasters; for I know their sorrows. Now therefore, behold, the cry of the children of Israel is come unto me: and I have also seen the oppression wherewith the Egyptians oppress them" (Exodus 3:7, 9).

God also stated His intentions for the Israelites: "And I am come down to deliver them out of the hand of the Egyptians, and to bring them up out of that land unto a good land and a large, unto a land flowing with milk and honey" (Exodus 3:8). God then gave the means by which His plan would be carried out: "Come now therefore, and I will send thee unto Pharaoh, that thou mayest bring forth my people the children of Israel out of Egypt" (Exodus 3:10).

## God Uses Men

Israel's deliverance was waiting for the development of a leader that God could use. And such a man was in the divine process of preparation.

God takes His time in molding the character of a leader and preparing him for a task. The need for spiritual leadership can develop quickly, but it requires years to form a leader. Moses was in preparation for eighty years. Joseph was twenty years in training despite the fact it took only a few hours for him to be elevated from a prisoner to the Prime Minister.

God is vitally concerned with the development of leadership before His people are allowed to enter into His provision. Israel waited in exile, for example, while God prepared Nehemiah to lead them out. Before there was ever a church in existence, Jesus had already selected and was training a band of disciples for leadership. God prepared the ministry before the church was established.

## Why Leadership?

People are God's main concern. The work of the kingdom of God is a "people business." God's people are more important to Him than positions of leadership. It is because of the people's needs that God calls leaders.

God's great love for people was His motivation to call leaders into the work of the kingdom. He once saw the people as sheep having no shepherd, wandering without direction (Matthew 9:36). He was deeply moved with compassion. Christ then issued a call into the harvest because of the listless condition of the people. "Pray ye therefore the Lord of the harvest, that he will send forth labourers into his harvest" (Matthew 9:38).

## The Gift of Leadership

All the gifts and talents given to God-called leaders are given to men for the benefit of God's people. In reality, leadership is God's gift to His people. He loves them so much that He provides leaders to govern, protect, and lead. Leaders are the channel through which He Himself can speak to His "anointed" and chosen people.

The creation of the ministry was the initiative of God. In fact, most scriptural leaders were busy with their own trades when God intercepted them and commissioned them to serve His people. Moses and David were tending their herds; many of the disciples were involved in their fishing enterprises; Matthew was conducting his tax collections. Each was called out and set apart for the purpose of leadership in God's kingdom. In describing the forerunner of Jesus Christ, the Apostle John wrote, "There was a man sent from God, whose name was John" (John 1:6). God still sends men today as gifts of leadership to His church.

When addressing the elders of Ephesus, Paul reminded them that their place of leadership was the choice of the Holy Ghost. "Take heed therefore unto yourselves, and to all the flock, over the which the Holy Ghost hath made you overseers, to feed the church of God, which he hath purchased with his own blood" (Acts 20:28). When leaders became either too haughty or discouraged, they were to remember that their place of leadership was appointed by God. Furthermore, the people should be reminded that God gave them leaders.

The Apostle Paul mentioned this gift of leadership in his letter to the Ephesian church. In discussing the mighty redemptive works of Christ, Paul wrote that He gave gifts unto men. (See Ephesians 4:7-8.) Paul's thoughts flowed right into the ministry as God's gift to the church: "And he gave some, apostles; and some, prophets; and some, evangelists; and some, pastors and teachers" (Ephesians 4:11).

The Apostle Paul pointed out that these ministries

were given to the church for its perfection or completion (verse 12). The word translated "perfecting" is the Greek word *katartismos,* which can be translated, "complete furnishing." The ministry is given to the church to fully furnish and equip the people so they will not be cast about with every wind of doctrine, and they will be able to fulfill their individual ministries as members of the body of Christ.

If the ministry is the agency that God has chosen to mature and equip the church, then without the God-ordained ministry the church cannot be mature and equipped to reach the lost world for Christ.

## Accepting the Ministry

There are those who find it difficult to accept another human being as their spiritual leader. This has been a problem from the time of the call of Moses. After his ordination and anointing, Moses embarked upon a powerful spiritual ministry. Nonetheless, it was difficult for his older sister Miriam to fully acknowledge the hand of the Lord on her little brother's life. After all, hadn't she been his babysitter? Had she not helped care for him in his infancy? Who was he now to tell her what the Lord wanted her to do?

At one time she and her brother Aaron spoke against Moses. They felt it was time to put him in his place and remind him that God could speak to them as well as to him. What they had not reckoned with was the fact that God's anointing upon a man makes a great difference.

The anger of the Lord was kindled against Miriam because of her rebellion against the ministry God had given to Israel. The curse of leprosy came upon her, and she would have died in that condition if Moses had not interceded before the Lord in her behalf. Moses was no longer just her little brother; he was

God's anointed vessel given to the nation to lead them out of Egypt.

When God lays His hand on a person and calls that person to be a leader among His people, it changes some relationships. No longer was David just a little brother after God called him, but an anointed leader due honor. Joseph's relationship with his brothers changed dramatically when God elevated him to leadership over them. Even Christ's relationship with Joseph and Mary changed as God's call became apparent in His life. Jesus was no longer just the son of a carpenter.

The writer to the Hebrew Christians concluded his remarks to them with some strong admonitions concerning submission to the leadership structure established by God: "Obey them that have the rule over you, and submit yourselves: for they watch for your souls, as they that must give account, that they may do it with joy, and not with grief: for that is unprofitable for you" (Hebrews 13:17). To refuse to accept and submit to the direction of the ministry God has given the church is unprofitable. Not only does one become a rebel against God's authority when he rejects the ministry, he also becomes confused and lost without the direction of a leader.

When Jesus sent His disciples out, He gave them an important promise: "He that receiveth you receiveth me" (Matthew 10:40).

The Apostle Peter described those who despise authority as walking after the lust of the flesh, being presumptuous, self-willed, and not afraid to speak evil of dignities (II Peter 2:10). Apparently when people refuse the leadership that God has so graciously given to the church of His own volition, there are some resultant spiritual penalties. When men refuse the spiritual umbrella of protection God provides them, they are exposed to every spiritual danger and are placed in a very precarious position.

What if some of the Israelites had decided that Moses was taking too much authority and they could leave Egypt any time they wanted? Suppose they refused his instructions and devised their own plan? First of all, their firstborn sons would have suffered death because of their rebellion. Secondly, they would not have been able to cross the Red Sea until the man of God with the rod of the Lord in his hand was present. In fact, most who left Egypt never made it to the Promised Land because of their continual rebellion against Moses' leadership.

## The Ministry Leads

With few exceptions, people seldom rise higher in spiritual dimensions than the level of their leadership. A close study of the nation of Israel demonstrates that fact. The same people came under various types of leaders and a wide variety of results was produced. Under the strong leadership of Joshua, Israel was a conquering force. But during the period of the judges, when every man did that which was right in his own eyes, the land was overrun with enemies. Later, during the period of the kings, the nation experienced the rise and fall of revival in direct proportion to the caliber of their leadership.

The history of revival in the church has shown that there is always a key individual that God calls out to initiate renewal. He has used John the Baptist, Peter, Paul, Frank Ewart, A. D. Urshan, C. P. Kilgore and many others to bring revival to the church. Strong leadership is necessary for revival.

## Saved by Preaching

God chose a very foolish method by human standards to redeem the lost from sin. Paul said, "It pleased God by the foolishness of preaching to save them that believe" (I Corinthians 1:21). "For whosoever shall call upon the name of the Lord shall be saved. How then shall they call on him in whom they have not believed? and how shall they believe in him of whom they have not heard? and how shall they hear without a preacher?" (Romans 10:13-14).

Paul's statements are strongly supportive of the ministry as God's gift to the church. Men cannot be saved without faith in God, and they cannot exercise faith in Him if they have not been exposed to the gospel. Paul tied the salvation of the lost with the necessity of a preacher.

The illustration of Cornelius is a beautiful picture of a devout man of prayer seeking for truth. (See Acts 10.) As Cornelius was in his devotions, an angel of the Lord came to him. The angel did not preach the gospel to him but instead gave him the necessary instructions on how he could contact Simon Peter. Salvation came as the result of the message of the preacher. As great as the visit of the angel must have been, the entrance of the preacher into Cornelius' home was even greater.

## Roles of the Ministry

In the twelfth chapter of the first letter to the Corinthians, the Apostle Paul wrote concerning the unity of the body of Christ and compared it to the human body. Although there are many members of the body, they are interdependent and united to function in coordination. "Now ye are the body of Christ, and members in particular" (I Corinthians 12:27). Paul further stated, "And God hath set some in the church, first apostles, secondarily prophets, thirdly teachers, after that miracles, then gifts of healings, helps, governments, diversities of tongues" (I Corinthians 12:28).

The unity and coordinated work of the body of Christ is directly connected to the acceptance of the ministry God has set in the church. Paul wrote concerning this multi-faceted ministry in his letter to the Ephesian church as well. (See Ephesians 4:11-12.) These various ministries have been given to the church to minister to its many needs. When the ministry is given its proper place of authority and respect in the church, there can be revival and unity.

All of these various roles of the ministry listed in both I Corinthians 12:28 and Ephesians 4:11 are still operative in the church today. The very definitions of the terms found in these passages of Scripture identify definite works of Christ that continue yet in His church. God gave these ministries of apostles, prophets, evangelists, pastors and teachers to the church, and there is no indication that He ever withdrew them. (See Ephesians 4:11-12.) Since there is no verse of Scripture that informs us otherwise, we must conclude that the body of Christ today is equipped with the same ministries that existed in the original New Testament church.

Sometimes spiritual ministries that God has placed in the church are not recognized because these people do not carry the title of "apostle" or "prophet." But these are not elected offices, nor are they titles to be lightly bestowed on leaders. It is the nature of work that one does, not the office he holds, that identifies a man's ministry. Some leaders in the church world may hold certain titles of this nature but might not have the spiritual authority or evidence of work that signify these offices.

There are twelve founding apostles of the church (Ephesians 2:20; Revelation 21:14). These men are listed in Acts 1:13, 26. But these men were not the only ones who were called apostles. It is known certainly that Paul was an apostle. Barnabas was called an apostle (Acts 14:4, 14). Andronicus and Junia, whom some believe were among the seventy Jesus had sent out, were called apostles (Romans 16:7). Even Jesus Christ himself was called an apostle (Hebrews 3:1).

The word *apostle* seems to have been given to outstanding spiritual leaders who possessed a special anointing, especially when opening new fields to the gospel. The word simply means "one sent forth with a commission to do a particular task." An awareness of those who have ministered in the modern church would cause us to recognize that some foreign and home missionaries, as well as other powerful leaders, have actually functioned in the office of an apostle at times.

The same principles apply to the office of the prophet, one who is especially anointed to give God's people spiritual direction regarding a particular circumstance. The Old Testament people of God had prophets; the New Testament church also had prophets, such as Barnabas, Simeon, Lucius, Manaen, Agabus, and perhaps the daughters of Philip. (See Acts 13:1; 21:9, 10.) If God gave those ancient people the office of a prophet, and Paul wrote that it was part of the inheritance gift to the church, then it is certainly possible that God will use some modern church leaders in that capacity.

## Continuing Ministry

The statement, "And God hath set some in the church," denotes continual action (I Corinthians 12:28). What He gave to the Early Church, He has given to His people in these last days. The spiritual power and authority the Early Church exercised is available today. But in order for this gift to be operative, Christians must recognize it, identify it, and claim it from the hand of God.

Several times in his writings, Paul used the phrase "for your sakes." Paul wrote, "Though he was rich, yet for your sakes he became poor, that ye through his poverty might be rich" (II Corinthians 8:9). Of course, he wrote of Jesus Christ. The spiritual condition of the people compelled Christ to strip Himself of all honor and come to their level in order to save them.

In the context of discussing his role of the ministry to the church, Paul said that his ministry was given to the church "for your sakes." (See II Corinthians 4:15; I Thessalonians 1:5.) The same God who stripped Himself for the sake of the people, and came as their Savior, gave those that He had redeemed the ministry because of their continual need of leadership.

Fortunate are the people who can recognize the biblical ministry as a gift from God. The ministry has always been occupied by fallible people such as Moses, Peter, and Paul. They needed a Savior like everyone else. But God, in His love for His church, has laid His anointing hand upon fellow human beings today as well as then, and we are admonished to accept them in their spiritual office as a gift from God.

The burden of the ministry is epitomized by these words from the heart of the apostle as he pled with the church: "Be ye followers of me, even as I also am of Christ" (I Corinthians 11:1).

### Test Your Knowledge

#### True or False

_____ 1. God's method of government is called democracy.

_____ 2. Moses was in preparation for leadership for eighty years.

_____ 3. People are God's main concern.

_____ 4. Leadership is a gift to the church.

_____ 5. God gave the ministry to the church because it is perfect.

_____ 6. God judged Miriam's rebellion against her brother, Moses.

_____ 7. Those who receive or reject the disciples of Jesus Christ actually receive or reject Christ.

_____ 8. People are saved through singing, not preaching.

_____ 9. Preaching is foolishness.

_____ 10. It is the nature of work that one does, not the office he holds, which identifies his ministry.

## Apply Your Knowledge

Do something special for your pastor, pastors, or pastoral staff. There are many things you could do as a good gesture of appreciation—prepare a meal, take them out to dinner, send a card or letter, etc. It is not the lavishness of the act done, but the sincerity of the appreciation which is most appreciated.

All leaders like to be appreciated and told so once in awhile. Thoughtful and considerate church members will encourage ministers to be thoughtful and considerate.

## Expand Your Knowledge

Read the Scriptures for chapter eight before continuing. The Word of God is strong and sure and will accomplish every purpose for which it is sent.

# The Bible—
# Our Sure Foundation

*Thy word have I hid in mine heart, that I might not sin against thee.*

*Psalm 119:11*

---
**Start With the Scriptures**

Deuteronomy 4:2-14;
  6:6-9; 30:11-14
Joshua 1:8
Psalm 19:7-11
Isaiah 28:16; 55:10-11

Matthew 7:24-29
I Corinthians 3:10-15
II Timothy 3:15-17
Hebrews 6:13-20
II Peter 1:15-21

---

## The Bible's Message to Me

"Jesus loves me, this I know...." So begins a favorite song of Sunday school children. But how do I know Jesus loves me? How do I know that what I feel is Jesus loving me when I worship in church? How do I know that the sensation I feel and attribute to Jesus' love is really any different from the thrill of a snow skier as he soars off a jump platform, or the tingling spine of a patriot who snaps a salute as

"Old Glory" glides by, accompanied by the brassy strains of "Stars and Stripes Forever," or the breathless awe of honeymooners holding each other's hands as they peer through the mist of the thundering Niagara Falls?

We can know Jesus loves us! The children's chorus points the way—"For the Bible tells me so." The Bible tells us of the God who loves, and it is the Bible that tells us how we can experience that love.

But have we really answered the question of how we can *know?* Haven't we really pushed back the issue one step, from Jesus and His love to the truth of the Bible? Do we have any reasons to believe the Bible, to place our confidence in its truth, to build on it, knowing it is our sure foundation?

In this chapter you will see why the Bible deserves our complete confidence as the Word of God. The testimony of the Bible itself, along with the teaching of Jesus about the Bible, will both be considered. Ways in which the breadth of human experience and knowledge gives further testimony to the divine inspiration of the Bible will also be examined.

## The Old Testament Witness

Christians commonly cite verses of Scripture in the New Testament to show that the Bible is God's inspired Word. However, the Old Testament also contains a number of instances in which men of God affirmed that what they declared and wrote came by the command of God Himself.

When God called Moses to Mount Sinai, He gave him the Law engraved on tablets of stone. These tablets were finally placed in the Ark of the Covenant as a constant reminder that God had indeed spoken to His people. His laws had been written down for them and their posterity.

This Word that God had given Israel was not to

be treated lightly. It was not the word of man, it was the Word of God. As Moses instructed Israel in God's precepts, he warned them: "Ye shall not add unto the word which I command you, neither shall ye diminish ought from it, that ye may keep the commandments of the LORD your God which I command you" (Deuteronomy 4:2). He continued, "I have taught you statutes and judgments, even as the LORD my God commanded me" (verse 5).

Moses reminded the people that he was not the only one to whom God had spoken. All of them had heard the voice of God as He had spoken to them from Mount Horeb. They had seen the mountain burning with fire, heard the thundering voice as God spoke to them out of the fire: "Ye heard the voice of the words" (Deuteronomy 4:12).

Joshua added his witness when he testified that God had also spoken to him and had confirmed all he had said to Moses: "Be thou strong and very courageous, that thou mayest observe to do according to all the law, which Moses my servant commanded thee: turn not from it to the right hand or to the left" (Joshua 1:7). God then promised him that if he would "observe to do according to all that is written therein" he would prosper and have success.

God spoke to Samuel when he was but a child and told him of the judgments He would bring upon Eli the priest and upon his house. Later, Eli's sons were killed in battle and Eli himself fell and died of a broken neck when he heard that the Ark of God had been captured by the Philistines (I Samuel 3:11-13). King Solomon terminated the priesthood of the descendants of Eli when he removed Abiathar "that he might fulfil the word of the LORD, which he spake concerning the house of Eli in Shiloh" (I Kings 2:27).

Christians believe the Old Testament brings God's Word to them because they believe that men such as Moses, Joshua, and Samuel told the truth when they said that God had spoken His Word to them. Others may reject the claims of these men but if one rejects, for instance, Moses' word, he necessarily accuses Moses either of lying or of being hopelessly deluded about the most important experiences that shaped his life. To have a case against such a witness, the skeptic must produce evidence to cast doubt on the honesty or sanity of these leaders of Israel.

## The New Testament Witness to the Old Testament

The New Testament writers believed that the Old Testament was, in its entirety, the Word of God. "All scripture is given by inspiration of God" (II Timothy 3:16). "All scripture" referred to the Hebrew Bible, which is the Old Testament. When Peter reminded believers of the truthfulness of Christ's message, he appealed to the prophecies of the Old Testament, prophecies which "came not in old time by the will of man: but holy men of God" who spoke as they were moved upon by the Holy Ghost (II Peter 1:21).

Several other New Testament verses use a variety of expressions such as "scriptures" (Acts 17:2, 11; 18:28), "Word of God" (Romans 9:6; Hebrews 4:12), and "the law" (Acts 25:8; Romans 2:14), revealing the unanimous conviction of the earliest Christians that the entire Old Testament was the Word of God.

Every writer of the New Testament quoted, alluded to, or depended upon the words of the Old Testament as the foundation upon which the full revelation of Jesus Christ was established. No passage in the New Testament argues with or attempts to correct a command, a prophecy, or a historical statement made in the Old Testament. On the contrary, the message of the New Testament clearly confirms what God had spoken through "holy men of old." He fulfilled every one of these promises in Jesus Christ.

## Jesus' Witness to the Old Testament

What did Jesus believe about the Old Testament? Without any hesitation, He completely endorsed it as the Word of God. He defeated Satan's temptations by wielding the Old Testament Scriptures, declaring unequivocally: "It is written" (Luke 4:4-12).

He defined His own ministry in terms of the Old Testament. Speaking in the Nazareth synagogue, Jesus presented Himself as the Anointed One spoken of by Isaiah (Luke 4:16-21). Jesus taught that the Old Testament existed to testify of Him (John 5:39).

## Jesus Commissioned the New Testament

If Christians are assured that the Old Testament is God's Word by the triple witness of "holy men of old," the writers of the New Testament, and Jesus Christ Himself, what assures them that the New Testament also is nothing less than the Word of God? If a person believes in Jesus as Lord and Christ, he already has that assurance. By choosing and commissioning disciples and apostles to bear witness of Him, Jesus authenticated the New Testament even before it was written (Matthew 28:19, 20; Mark 16:15; Luke 24:46-49).

Who could be better qualified to attest to the truth of the ministry, death, and resurrection of Jesus than those who were by His side during the few years of those events? The original disciples and apostles of the Lord were witnesses to Him in a unique way; not only were they witnesses to the salvation which Jesus gives to people of every age, but they, unlike Christians today, saw the Lord Himself open blind eyes, cause the dead to live, and force evil spirits to flee. They heard His words when He spoke and they were there when He was arrested, crucified, and buried. And just as surely as they knew He had died, they also knew that He arose. They saw Him, touched Him, ate with Him, and saw Him ascend back into Heaven. They could believe because they had seen (I John 1:1-3).

John, Matthew, and all the other New Testament writers wrote to those who could not witness His mighty works but could believe through the witness of those who had been there. Jesus prayed for those "who shall believe on me" through the words of His first disciples. He emphasized that the witness of these men and women would be the way that the truth about Him would reach around the world (John 17:20).

The New Testament, then, is the permanent recorded witness of the earliest disciples and apostles of Jesus Christ. The church knows this witness is authoritative because it was commissioned directly by Jesus Christ. Thus, Christians have the assurance of an authority no less than our Lord God that the New Testament also is fully a product of His mind and will. It is a sure foundation upon which they can build for eternity!

## The Testimony of Fulfilled Prophecy

One of the most intriguing testimonies to the divine authorship of the Bible is the abundance of fulfilled prophecy contained within its pages. Fulfilled prophecy powerfully demonstrates the sureness of God's Word. One example already mentioned is that of the prophecy given to young Samuel. In another case, God warned Israel that if they worshiped other gods, He would withhold rain from their land (Deuteronomy 11:16-17). This happened during the days of King Ahab: "And Elijah the Tishbite. . .said unto Ahab, As the LORD God of Israel liveth, before whom I stand, there shall not be dew nor rain these years, but according to my word" (I Kings 17:1).

In the days of Jeroboam, king of Israel, a prophet from Judah came to the altar where Jeroboam was burning incense. "And he cried against the altar in the word of the LORD, and said, O altar, altar, thus saith the LORD; Behold, a child shall be born unto the house of David, Josiah by name; and upon thee shall he offer the priests of the high places that burn incense upon thee, and men's bones shall be burnt upon thee" (I Kings 13:1-2).

This prophecy was fulfilled 350 years later! A king was born of David's lineage and his name was Josiah. He came to Israel as the prophet had predicted, ordered the priests to remove all the vessels dedicated to Baal and had them burned. He broke down the altars erected to Baal, destroyed the groves dedicated to his worship, and broke all his images. "And he slew all the priests of the high places that were there upon the altars, and burned men's bones upon them, and returned to Jerusalem" (II Kings 23:20).

The closing verses of II Chronicles describe another instance of prophecy fulfilled: the captivity of Judah by Nebuchadnezzar, king of Babylon. The passage of Scripture gives the reason for the captivity: "To fulfill the word of the LORD by the mouth of Jeremiah, until the land had enjoyed her sabbaths: for as long as she lay desolate she kept sabbath, to fulfill threescore and ten years" (II Chronicles 36:21).

Centuries before, God had instructed Israel to allow their land to rest one year out of every seven (Exodus 23:11). He added that if they failed to obey this injunction, they would be judged for their disobedience (Leviticus 26:33-34). For 490 years, Israel failed to observe the sabbatical year. Seventy sabbatical years had been ignored. Surely, after all this time, God would not remember their disobedience of His Word. But He did, and He drove them from the land as He had warned Moses.

## The Testimony of Archeology

A number of historic records preserved in the Bible have aided scholars in identifying ancient empires. Some of them have used the Bible as a guide to locate the site of a city covered over with many layers of debris and dirt. These are commonly known as "tells" or mounds. "Excavations at Shiloh, Gibeah, Megiddo, Samaria, and other Palestinian sites have fully corroborated the Biblical notices of these cities" (Merrill F. Unger in *Archeology and the Old Testament).*

There was a day when many scholars scoffed at some of the names of monarchs mentioned in the Bible, but not so today. Archeologists Unger, Dougherty, and Gadd, all cite references to Belshazzar, the last king of Babylon through the discoveries of archeologists in recent years. Prior to these findings, scholars were fully convinced the Bible was in error when it stated that Belshazzar was king of Babylon at the time of its conquest by the Medes and Persians. Historical records all insisted that Nabonidus, and not Belshazzar, was king at the time of Babylon's fall. However, the conflict was resolved when "Evidence was uncovered not only indicating Belshazzar's association with Nabonidus on the throne but also demonstrating that during the last part of his reign the latter resided in Arabia and left the conduct of the kingdom of Babylon to...Belshazzar" (*Ibid.,* p. 16).

A similar case is that of Sargon, king of Assyria, mentioned in Isaiah 20:1. Until the discovery of Sargon's palace by Paul Emile Botta and subsequent research by the Oriental Institute of the University of Chicago, some scholars thought the Bible was in error since there was no historical record of this king. Again, the archeological work of Botta and others demonstrated the truth of the Bible. As a result of extensive research, Sargon is now one of the best known of all the Assyrian kings! He reigned from 722-705 B.C. and was the king who took the Northern Kingdom of Israel captive in 721 B.C.

The more research man does in countries mentioned in the Bible, the more he discovers the truth of God's Word.

## The Testimony of Personal Experience

It has been noted the way in which the New Testament helps fulfill the commission Jesus gave His apostles to bear witness of Him throughout the earth. This leads to another testimony to the sure foundation the Bible provides. The New Testament records the great results which accompanied the preaching and teaching of the apostles. Within Acts alone, in just a few verses, the church grew by 3,000 on one day with another 5,000 added soon after. The Word of God was effective. However, this Word was not only effective then, but wherever the Bible has been preached, similar results have been achieved. Peter guided some 3,000 to salvation on the Day of Pentecost, but how many more hundreds of thousands have responded through the ages to his command to "Repent, and be baptized every one of you in the name of Jesus Christ for the remission of sins, and ye shall receive the gift of the Holy Ghost"? (Acts 2:38).

If you have obeyed the apostolic command and have received the promised Holy Spirit, you have a biblically-based personal experience which testifies that the Bible is true, that it is as much the Word of God today as when it was first uttered 2,000 years ago! You know by experience that man apart from Christ is utterly sinful and that without Christ, man has no hope of deliverance from sin. You know by experience that the Bible's promise of forgiveness of sin and new life in the Holy Ghost is real.

Consequently, you have every reason in the world to believe that everything else it proclaims is true as well. You know the joy of being a child of God, and that knowledge quickens your faith that Jesus Christ is coming back again, soon, to complete the redemption He has begun in you.

## Obeying the Word

When a person has heard the Word with his heart, and the Holy Spirit has guided the light of truth into the recesses of his being, he then reveals by his response whether or not the Bible is his sure foundation. Should he be a hearer only who does not put into practice the teachings of God's Word, he deceives himself. However, if he practices the precepts of God's Word daily, he will be participating in the building of a great house, "an habitation of God through the Spirit" (Ephesians 2:22). This Word will enable a person to stand through all adversity. John promised that he who does the will of God will abide forever (I John 2:17).

When we hear and read the Word and practice it on a regular, consistent basis, we also discover two blessed results:

- We know by personal experience and the con-

vincing assurance of the Spirit that the Bible is true.
- We know in increasingly personal, intimate ways that Jesus loves us!

These things—the most important things—we can know "for the Bible tells me so."

## Test Your Knowledge

### Witnesses of God's Word

Can you find these witnesses?

| Moses | Peter | Matthew |
| Joshua | Paul | Fulfilled Prophecy |
| Samuel | Every Writer | Archeology |
| Solomon | Jesus Christ | Personal Experience |
| Elijah | John | |

```
C I T H O M H W O A B A F I C G B I
Y C E H P O R P D E L L I F L U F Z
H V X Y G A J O H N G U S P R U S M
K X T O K W R R P P N Q S W W E L D
W K D C K Z T C D K V D A R O V S U
O M X J P X U M H A B J Q S G E U P
E C N E I R E P X E L A N O S R E P
K A Z X P N I J I K O K K P B Y R T
P G L M P E O X N P D L S L E W D J
A Y H Y O E L M M I Y O O J O R U M
U Z Y J D S T I O A K F T G U I A F
L Y L V O H E E J L H X W J Y T L Q
K P A E D S O S R A O N T Q T E E M
F E D B U D H S J O H S T H R R H P
K Y A C H M N U Y R E S E V W Q W Y
R W Y Y M B A F A K W W B S I E T W
L F A J C J W S S F N M L O X A O Y
T S I R H C S U S E J C V W L V T I
```

## Apply Your Knowledge

There is no other source of power, comfort, encouragement and strength in our lives like God's Word—the Bible. The Bible is a great book, but it is much more than a book. It is the road map to Heaven for all people who will follow it.

An excellent program for reading the Bible through each year is the BREAD program—Bible Reading Enriches Any Day. A chart to help you maintain your daily Bible reading is available by writing the General Sunday School Division, 8855 Dunn Road, Hazelwood, MO 63042.

## Expand Your Knowledge

Prepare for chapter nine by reading the Scriptures listed at the beginning of the chapter. These will lay a foundation of thought for the material covered concerning "praise." Excellent resources for further information are *Pentecostal Worship* by Gary D. Erickson and *A Look at Pentecostal Worship* from the Word Aflame Publications elective series. These books can be ordered from the Pentecostal Publishing House, 8855 Dunn Road, Hazelwood, MO 63042-2299.

# Praise and Worship

*Enter into his gates with thanksgiving, and into his courts with praise: be thankful unto him, and bless his name.*

*Psalm 100:4*

---

### Start With the Scriptures

Psalm 5:7; 22:22;
   24:3-6; 27:4; 63:1
Ecclesiastes 5:1
Isaiah 40:31
Luke 4:8

John 4:23
Ephesians 5:19-20
Hebrews 10:25
I Peter 2:5

---

Someone once stated that praise is the intangible commodity that works to make good men better and bad men worse.

This statement has been proven true in the experience of life. Everyone has had the opportunity to observe firsthand the effects of praise on those around him. Some people have been motivated to high achievement by kind words while others have almost been destroyed by the same honors. Praise is not a garment worn well by all to whom it is given.

Yet man was made to both praise and be praised, and when it comes to honoring one another, most people are quite proficient. Everyone has his heroes and not only knows how to, but does, exalt them.

The average person spends much time praising. He readily notes the excellence in a book or a car, a home or a boat, and freely gives praise that at times may border on worship.

If this be true, how rewarding it would be if people were more sensitive to notice the perfect beauty of Christ, His splendid creation, and His wonderful plan for salvation. What a shame it is that some people are keenly aware of the kindnesses of others and freely compliment, thank, and praise them, and all the while ignore the richer blessings from God's hand.

## Purpose of Man

For a man to miss the opportunity to praise and worship God is for that man to miss his very purpose for existence. The Psalms often put forth a rapturous call to worship and a clear answer to the age-old question, "What is the primary reason for the creation of man?" The answer is simple: "Humanity was created to be worshipers of God."

Man was not created as a result of any external necessity in God, for the Lord has no external needs. He is self-sufficient. God did not, nor will He ever, need man in the sense of a child needing a guardian to protect, provide, counsel or empower. He is omniscient, omnipotent and omnipresent. He does not need man as a car needs gas, a plane needs wings or a boat depends upon an oar to function properly.

The truth remains that man is the product of an internal desire in God, and man can better minister to God's internal desire than any other part of His creation. God is perfect, pure, infinitely loving and abounding in mercy and has no external needs that He cannot meet for Himself. However, internally He has a "God-sized" desire to be recognized for His magnificent greatness. He wanted some creature that was capable of noticing what a wonderful God He is and was then capable of choosing to know, admire and honor Him. God has a great desire to be loved.

Following the Friday night that Muhammed Ali won the world heavyweight boxing crown for an unprecedented third time, he was observed in the New Orleans airport. Ali entered, surrounded by a great entourage of fans and staff members who traveled with him. He did not travel alone. He was more than willing to pay for extra airfares, rooms and meals just to have the companionship of some old-time friends who would watch him work, praise him for a job well done and then share with him the victory, his crowning glory!

Why is it that a politician running for public office arranges to have a suite filled with close friends and a campaign headquarters packed with staff and supporters on the night of the election? Why does he desire to have loyal family members nearby as he awaits the outcome of the voting? He realizes that a victory, no matter how large it may be, is lacking a major ingredient of completeness if the victor has no one on hand with whom he can share it. Therefore, his internal needs cause him to make sure he is surrounded with loyalists who will offer praise in what he hopes will be his finest hour.

For this reason God made men to share in the glory of His handiwork. He has an internal desire for someone to notice the ongoing work of creation and then praise Him for it. He longs for men to perceive His handiwork and proclaim His excellence. He wants men to recognize and praise His many attributes.

Everyone has something that God wants, even needs, for the personal reward of His handiwork to be complete—pure praise. He wants someone with whom He can share His handiwork.

## Complete Worship

There are two qualities that must be joined together for worship to be complete—knowledge and feeling. No man can truly worship another apart from personal knowledge of that individual's greatness. One must be personally knowledgeable of the other's strengths if he is to be really sincere in praise.

True worship of God can only spring from a knowing relationship. A Christian must take time to know Him in order to be able to perfectly praise Him. Praise apart from knowledge is empty and convinces no one, not even oneself, of God's faithfulness.

After a person comes to know God, he must build his praises around what he knows to be true about Him and mix with those praises the feelings of his heart. We should not worship God because of what we feel, but because of what we know. However, feeling and emotion must be involved. It is the feeling and emotion wrapped around the words "I love you" that makes the heart of a person glad. One who goes through the motions, says all the right words, but feels nothing in his heart does not touch the heart of God.

A person may wonder: "How then do I go about praising God? I know how to praise men and do. Now I realize that God also desires, even needs, my praise for His joy to be complete. I also realize that my praise must consist of that which I personally know to be true of the character of God and should be offered with much emotion, feelings. . .heart. But how do I go about giving my worthy God the praise He deserves?"

## Seven Words for Praise

The Bible teaches how to manifest praise unto God.

In a book entitled *Praise, Faith in Action,* author Charles Trombley reveals that the Old Testament uses seven Hebrew words to portray the entire biblical portrait of praise. Let us consider them and enlarge our understanding as to how we can physically express our adoration to God!

*The first Hebrew word for praise is **yadah**, the root of which means to throw out the hand, the extended hand, or to worship with the extended hand.* The lexicon further shows that the opposite meaning of the word is to bemoan. It speaks of the wringing of the hands. In other words, one who fails to lift his hands as a part of victorious worship may in fact be wringing them in whimpering defeat.

When Jehoshaphat found his nation under seige by the surrounding nations, he called upon the priests to lead his troops into battle. He knew that he had no military might to depend on to deliver him, so he devised a plan whereby the priests would call on God through praise! "And the Levites, of the children of the Kohathites. . .went out before the army, and to say, Praise [*yadah*] the LORD; for his mercy endureth forever" (II Chronicles 20:19, 21). The priests went before the enemy, lifting their hands with all their strength unto God to show their dependence upon Him and shouting that His mercy endures forever. They were in essence saying, "Lord, we know we are outnumbered, but we are not afraid for we know we are Your children. We are depending on You and believing in Your power to deliver us! Here we stand trusting in You!" What happened? They praised (*yadah*) themselves to victory!

When Christians are outnumbered and facing certain defeat, not knowing where to turn, they may begin to praise *yadah* God for deliverance. They can throw their hands up with power toward the heavens. In the face of the enemy one can show his utter dependence on the Lord and thank Him for His everlasting mercy that will deliver from the present problem. "Lift up your hands in the sanctuary, and bless the LORD" (Psalm 134:2).

*The next word used to describe praise is **towdah** which comes from the same root as did **yadah**.* Both words involve the raising of the hands but *towdah* includes even more. It is the modern Hebrew word for thanksgiving and speaks of an extension of the hand in avowal, acceptance and adoration. Sometimes it was used to thank the Lord for blessings already received, but at other times it was used to thank God in advance for blessings that had not yet come. It honors God by taking Him at His Word and refuses to question or doubt His promises. It is the offering of thanksgiving for, and rejoicing in, something that is guaranteed by His Word even before it has actually taken place. It has only been seen through "faith's eye."

"Towdah" praise is the throwing of the hands into the air in praise to God for what His Word has said He will do. It is also the throwing of the hand into the air in recognition of what He has already accomplished in one's life.

*A third Hebrew word used to define praise is **shabach** which simply means to address in a loud tone, to command, triumph, glory, to shout!* Praise does not have to be quiet and reserved. *Shabach* refers to shouting God's praises with a loud voice. A loudly shouted praise is very acceptable unto God! "O God, thou art my God; early will I seek thee: my soul thirsteth for thee, my flesh longeth for thee in a dry and thirsty land, where no water is; Because thy lovingkindness is better than life, my lips shall praise [*shabach*] thee. Thus will I bless thee while I live: I will lift up my hands in thy name" (Psalm 63:1, 3-4). One passage of Scripture admonishes a person to "Shout unto God with the voice of triumph" (Psalm 47:1). If a person feels that God has been so good to him that he hardly knows how to express it, then he can shout His praise with a loud voice. This praise is acceptable unto God. It is not only pleasing to God, but it is scriptural worship.

*The fourth word used for praise is **barak** meaning to kneel or bless God as an act of adoration.* There is something in every Christian that occasionally wants to bow low before the Lord in worship and prayer. This word is sometimes translated to mean "to bow down in a worshipful attitude or to bless God expecting to receive something." "For he shall deliver the needy when he crieth; the poor also, and him that hath no helper. He shall spare the poor and needy, and shall save the souls of the needy. He shall redeem their soul from deceit and violence; and precious shall their blood be in his sight. And he shall live, and to him shall be given of the gold of Sheba: prayer also shall be made for him continually; and daily shall he be praised [*barak*]" (Psalm 72:12-15).

Oh what a promise! Christians can bow before the Lord and expect something good to happen. This is not stooping to beg, but kneeling in expectant worship—praising God and looking for Him to fulfill the promises in His Word.

*Another term used to describe worship is **zamar** which literally means to touch the strings and is used in conjunction with instrumental worship.* Psalm 150 mentions a wide variety of instruments and encourages us to [*zamar*] touch the strings, and use them in praise. "Zamar" praise is rejoicing. The majority of the instruments listed are either percussion or rhythm reflecting a lot of volume and downbeat used to rejoice before the Lord.

*The sixth Hebrew word is **halal**.* This is a root word from which the praise word, hallelujah, is derived. It means to shine, to boast, to rave and to be clamorously foolish. This is the type of praise that is most often practiced when the church assembles together. Christians sing, boast in the goodness of the Lord and extol His greatness. They often become so involved in "bragging on Jesus" that they may appear to some listening to be clamorously foolish. This does not mean that worshipers act foolish; it is just that some observers may think they are. It is easy to become so thankful for and proud of Jesus that a person may act like a young lover so enraptured with the girl of his dreams that he cannot stop boasting of her day and night. Everything about her to him is a thing of beauty and he feels compelled to tell somebody.

*The final Hebrew word for praise is **tehillah** which means to sing, to laud.* "But thou art holy, O thou that inhabitest the praises [*tehillah*] of Israel" Psalm 22:3). It is in this type of praise that God manifests Himself. This does not mean that God manifests Himself in all singing. It is only when the singing comes from the heart and is properly directed toward God that the Lord is there.

Yet *tehillah* is more than singing. *Tehillah* is even more than spirited singing. It is singing in the Spirit songs that were not prepared or premeditated but flow forth in praise produced by the Holy Ghost.

This distinction between singing and *tehillah* could be seen when Israel began to "sing *and* to praise [*tehillah*]" causing the Lord to set ambushments against her enemies. (See II Chronicles 20:22.)

So it is seen that a person praises the Lord by lifting his hands in dependence upon Him and by lifting his hands in thanksgiving for what God has done and what He is going to do. God is praised by the touching of fingers to the strings and the instruments, by getting so carried away in boasting of His greatness that a person would appear to be clamorously foolish, and by shouting His goodness in a loud voice. A person can also praise God by kneeling quietly and bowing low before Him in expectation of His honoring the promises in His Word and by spirited singing and singing in the Spirit.

There are many ways in which a person may worship God, but ultimately it is not what one does in worship, but the motive behind his worship that is most important.

## Worship Because of Love

Every wife longs to be remembered in a romantic way occasionally by her husband. One day a certain man decided he would really thrill his wife's heart by surprising her with a dozen roses, a beautiful card and a sincere poem of his own composition. What enjoyment he had that morning as he picked up the flowers, purchased the card and produced the poem! By the time he finished he was actually excited, carried away with his wonderful expression of love.

He hurried home, arranged it all on the dining room table and anxiously awaited his wife's return from town. When he heard the car coming down the drive, he hid himself in the kitchen. He just knew that as soon as she had seen the bouquet and read the poem she would be rushing into his arms.

He listened as she entered the front door, spotted the flowers and exclaimed, "Oh, how pretty!" He smiled to himself as she carefully opened the letter and poem, sighing as she read aloud.

Suddenly, he stepped into full view of his happy bride and braced himself for the rush and the hug that was to come, but she didn't move even one step.

Instead, she kindly looked at him and asked, "Why did you do this?"

He knew that the answer he gave would determine how much or how little the flowers and the writing were going to mean. She didn't want to hear him say, "Well, I bought a new suit and thought this would be a nice peace offering to balance things out" or "I just read a book that said this was the way for a man to please his wife." Had he said these things the gifts would have meant nothing. What the lady most wanted to hear were these few words, "I did it because I love you." Only that special reason for the kindness could make it precious.

So it is with the Lord. When we work for and worship Him, He stands back to look for the motivation for our good deeds and praise. It is as though He pauses to ask after the offering of our sacrifice, "Why did you do that?" More than anything He wants to hear us respond, "Because I love You!"

He really does not want us to praise Him from fear of being lost if we do not, or out of a compelling sense of obligation and duty to Him in light of all He has done to purchase our salvation. He does not want us to praise Him because we have heard of Heaven and desire to enjoy its rewards! He waits to hear us say, "Lord, I have said all of this and performed all of these good works simply because I do really love You. I'm so happy You are my God!"

Let's worship! Let's do it because we love!

## Test Your Knowledge

1. The purpose of man is to _____.
2. God made men to share in the glory of His _____.
3. Complete worship requires both knowledge and _____.

Match each word with the correct definition.

_____ 4. Yadah    a. to sing, to laud
_____ 5. Towdah    b. kneel and bless God in worship or prayer
_____ 6. Shabach    c. worship with the extended hand
_____ 7. Barak    d. shout God's praise with a loud voice
_____ 8. Zamar    e. to rave, boast, or be clamorously foolish
_____ 9. Halal    f. extending hands in avowal and acceptance
_____ 10. Tehillah    g. to touch the strings with instrumental worship

## Apply Your Knowledge

Of all God's creations, man should be the first in praise and worship of God. Man is highest in intelligence; he should be highest in thanksgiving.

Make a concerted effort to worship God in all the various types of worship. We may not always feel like worshiping God, but we can always praise Him for that which we "know." You may be amazed how much better you will feel when you go ahead and worship God.

## Expand Your Knowledge

The following chapter is entitled "Spiritual Healing for the Church." Please read and study all the Scriptures for the lesson before going on. As you read the verses of Scripture, be sensitive to the needs of your own congregation. What things does your church need to have the kind of revival it wants? Perhaps *you* can be the key to sparking revival among your fellow members and hence bring healing and revival to your church.

# Spiritual Healing for the Church

*If my people, which are called by my name, shall humble themselves, and pray, and seek my face, and turn from their wicked ways; then will I hear from heaven, and will forgive their sin, and will heal their land.*

*II Chronicles 7:14*

---

### Start With the Scriptures

Deuteronomy 28
Psalm 80:3; 85:4
Jeremiah 3:22; 8:22
Lamentations 5:21
Hosea 14:4

Malachi 3:10-11; 4:2
Acts 10:38
Hebrews 5:11-14; 6:1-3
Jude 3-4, 16
Revelation 2:1-7

---

To say that things were not going well would have been an understatement! The children were all grown and gone from home. Finances had never been worse for Jim and Mary. They were "swimming" in debt, just trying to stay afloat as creditors hounded them daily. Jim was out of work and restless beyond endurance. To top it all off Mary had just left Jim and had filed for divorce.

Unfortunate though it may be, the above scenario has become all too common. Many traditional homes throughout the world are facing similar circumstances. Struggles, problems and tragedies have invaded the family unit and are leaving paths of destruction and devastation behind them.

Equally sobering is the realization that many of the same struggles and problems facing families are facing the church as well. How many congregations and their pastors have divorced and separated solely because problems had arisen, pressures were heavy, and revival simply did not exist? Just as divorce is not the answer for troubled marriages, neither is separation between church and pastor the solution for revival. Sometimes ministers and laymen alike are tempted to seek the easy way out of a troubling situation.

The thrilling truth is that there is spiritual healing available for any congregation that suffers from any spiritual malady. When Christians will sincerely examine themselves and their roles in the body of Christ, there can and will come spiritual renewal.

## Symptoms of Spiritual Sickness

More than ever before, many physicians are beginning to practice "preventative health care." In other words, rather than wait until their patients are sick and need immediate, emergency treatment, doctors are diagnosing possible health problems before they develop. This can spare the patient much of the trauma and anguish experienced through illness, and possibly even death.

Preventative health care can be practiced in the spiritual realm as well. Why wait until a congregation of believers becomes seriously ill spiritually before administering the proper treatment? Symptoms appear early and are signals that spiritual renewal is needed at once. Some of the common symptoms of spiritual disease should be considered at this point.

*A church needs revival when divisions exist among the members.* The word *revival* primarily means "the act of returning or restoring to consciousness or life." Revival is a renewal of awareness and spiritual vitality. To the church, revival means a return to the living patterns of the original apostolic church that Christ set in order. That means a return to unity.

When God breathed life into His church at Jerusalem on the Day of Pentecost, He established a body of believers who were closely knit together in unity. They were "all with one accord in one place" (Acts 2:1). From that birthing of the church even to this day unity has been a significant characteristic of God's children.

Divisions within a church are signs of spiritual decay. When a person's spirituality begins to wane, he gets out of step with others in the church and division results. In writing to the Corinthian church, a church torn with division and strife, the Apostle Paul urged, "that ye all speak the same thing, and that there be no divisions among you; but that ye be perfectly joined together in the same mind and in the same judgment" (I Corinthians 1:10).

*Another symptom of spiritual sickness is that the people are carnal and worldly.* When people become carnal, they lose sight of spiritual goals and become critical and sensitive. The thoughts and discussions of the people deteriorate when they become carnal.

Carnality manifests itself in numerous ways in a church. The Apostle Paul recognized the Corinthians' carnality by the divisions, strife and envy that existed among them (I Corinthians 3:3). Carnal people will tend to gossip about the problems of others rather than discuss the good news of Jesus Christ. Carnal individuals will seek after worldly fashions, develop rebellious attitudes, and will resent and hold grudges against those who try to help them. Carnality must be purged from the church lest sincere Christians become infected and destroyed.

*When a church congregation is not seeing lost people experience salvation, it needs spiritual healing.* The church exists as an "ark of safety" to redeem the lost from sin. As the body of Christ, the church stands with its spiritual arms open to those who need salvation and shelter.

Jesus Christ came to "seek and to save that which was lost" (Luke 19:10). During Christ's earthly ministry He healed the sick and lame, opened deaf ears and blind eyes, and raised the dead to life. He cleansed lepers, befriended the friendless and turned water into wine. But none of these miracles exhibited the purpose for which He came—they were merely benefits of His compassion and love for mankind. He came for one reason only and that was to restore to men spiritual life which was lost because of sin. (See John 10:10.) He came to save men from sin.

For the church to exist for any reason other than the salvation of the lost would be completely contrary to the purpose of its creation. "Repentance and the remission of sins should be preached in his name among all nations, beginning at Jerusalem (Luke 24:47).

*Apathy and a lack of a burden for the lost is another symptom of spiritual illness in the church.* When a church is not seeing souls born again, it is generally due to this malady—apathy. When Christians do not care about their neighbors' spiritual condition as they should, they will not be soulwinners.

The Early Church exhibited a tremendous burden for lost souls. "And they went forth, and preached every where, the Lord working with them" (Mark 16:20). (See also Acts 8:4.) They possessed such a burning compassion to win the lost that it was said of them they had "turned the world upside down" (Acts 17:6) and had filled Jerusalem with their doctrine (Acts 5:28). The Apostle Paul spread the gospel throughout Asia in the space of two years (Acts 19:10).

Active evangelism keeps the love of Christ for lost men coursing through the spiritual arteries of the church. It is true that "Where there is no vision, the people perish" (Proverbs 29:18)—they who are lost perish and they who have no vision perish. But where there is a vision and burden to do the work of God there is abundant life!

*When there is no manifestation of the Spirit in a church service, that church needs revival!* The Holy Spirit is the life of the church. When God breathed into Adam he became a living soul, and when the Holy Ghost fell on the disciples at Pentecost they became a living church!

God intended for His church to be "charged" with His power and presence that He could minister to the people through His church. (See chapter eleven.) He never designed the church to be cold, ritualistic, and without life. He devised the church to meet the needs of people—not merely pacify them.

God manifests Himself in numerous ways in a church service. If there is no such manifestation, the church should take inventory of the problem and take steps to allow the Holy Spirit free reign and control of the services.

*Finally, the lack of giving is a symptom of disease in the church.* It is holy and natural for a Christian to give of his finances to the work of God.

God set the pattern for Christianity by giving Himself as a sacrifice for sin. (See John 3:16; I John 3:16.) God is a giving God. He will withhold no good gift from those who walk uprightly (Psalm 84:11). In fact, every good gift comes from Him (James 1:17).

Since a man is created in God's image and God left

him an example of giving, he should give also when the Spirit of God dwells within him. Tithes and offerings are both types of biblical giving that a man owes to God. (See Malachi 3:8-10.) Not only is it required by God that men give to His kingdom, but He also promised He would pour out a blessing that a person could not even contain (Malachi 3:10).

## Balm in Gilead

If one or all of these spiritual maladies should happen to exist in a church, there is an answer—there is hope! God has provided healing for those who are sick.

During a time of Israel's unfaithfulness to God, the prophet Jeremiah wrote, "Is there no balm in Gilead; is there no physician there?" (Jeremiah 8:22). Indeed there was balm in Gilead. In fact, Gilead had become quite renowned for its medicinal balms— excellent for the healing of the body. Israel's lack of healing was not to be blamed on the lack of healing power (spiritual) nor the lack of a physician (Jehovah) to apply it. Any lack of healing they experienced was due to their failure to apply the cure prescribed by God's prophets.

God has also provided spiritual healing for the church. The cures are prescribed in God's Word and must be applied with faith

The atonement of Jesus Christ's death on Calvary purchased not only physical healing for the church, but spiritual healing as well. Isaiah wrote, "But he was wounded for our transgressions, he was bruised for our iniquities; the chastisement of our peace was upon him; and with his stripes we are healed" (Isaiah 53:5). Of the four areas of atonement mentioned, three referred specifically to spiritual healing or atonement. God was more concerned in the spiritual welfare of His children than the physical—not to ignore their physical health. Jesus often demonstrated His concern for the spiritual man, even over the physical man. (See Mark 2:1-5.)

## Revival Is the Answer

The therapy and prescription are the same for every symptom of spiritual disease—revival! When Chistians are awakened to their spiritual prowess and motivated to a spiritual renewal of life, spiritual growth and Christian maturity will result. Every symptom will disappear and new spiritual vitality will reign.

*Revival cleanses the heart.* The carnal nature is purged out. The old dead roots and branches of sin are once again clipped away from a Christian's heart. The spiritual heart of a man is renewed and given room to grow when revival comes.

*Revival changes attitudes.* When a man's attitudes become sour and diseased, his entire life is affected. There is a unique relationship between a person's attitudes and his actions. Wrong attitudes produce wrong actions; right attitudes produce right actions! As a man thinks in his heart so is he (Proverbs 23:7).

A revival atmosphere in the church will cause Christians to respond with healthy, positive attitudes toward God, church leaders, the unregenerated, and themselves. These positive attitudes toward the things of God cause positive actions and involvement in church programs and activities, which in turn can produce more revival.

*Revival motivates spiritual growth.* As the heart is continually cleansed and attitudes strengthened by revival, spiritual growth will result. Growth is sometimes a slow and tedious process. Some things require years of slow, continual growth before reaching maturity. It also takes time to grow into spiritual maturity. Mature Christians are not made overnight—it takes time.

In order for plants to grow, the right combination of light, food, and water are necessary. Certain elements are also needed to institute spiritual growth and maturity. Revival contains all the necessary ingredients to motivate spiritual growth.

## The Way of Revival

A prescription designed to cure spiritual disease is only valuable if it is applied in actual therapy. Christians must not only assess their spiritual deficiencies and determine a course of therapy, but they should also begin actual rehabilitation.

One might say, "I know I have a problem and I know that revival is the cure, but how do I have revival?" Covered below are some steps of action to take which will bring revival to a church and hence, spiritual healing.

*Prayer and fasting.* Without a doubt these should top the list of steps to revival. They simply cannot be emphasized too much.

Prayer was evidently very important to God, for He desired His house to be called a house of prayer (Isaiah 56:7; Matthew 21:13). Even Jesus, though God wrapped in flesh, prayed often to the Father. According to Jesus, prayer and fasting were the only elements that could bind the power of the enemy and bring deliverance. (See Matthew 17:14-21.) (For more information on prayer refer to chapter three.)

Fasting must not be forgotten. It is an essential key to self-discipline of the flesh and natural man in order to be fully submitted to the Spirit. Fasting does not change God, for He does not change. (See Malachi 3:6; James 1:17.) Fasting changes the participant and helps him to keep his flesh subject to God's Spirit and His will.

*Faithfulness.* Each member being faithful to God's

house and service will help prepare a church for revival. "Moreover it is required in stewards, that a man be found faithful" (I Corinthians 4:2). God will only entrust revival to those He can depend on. Faithfulness is dependability.

Another element of faithfulness is consistency. When a Christian is consistent in the life he lives to the degree that he is dependable, then he is faithful!

If a businessman is faithful to his business and there is a need for the product he produces, he will prosper. There can be no question that there is tremendous need for the product offered by the church. If those who operate the business of the church will be diligent and faithful in any circumstance, the church and its members will be blessed and prosper. (See Proverbs 28:20.) Revival is available for those who will faithfully and diligently seek it.

*Giving.* Consistent giving to the work of God will help initiate revival. Giving of one's financial substance is in the plan of God for basically three reasons:

- It tests a Christian's faith in God.
- It is an expression of a Christian's love, devotion and commitment to God.
- It finances the earthly work of God.

God will bless those who give to His cause. He will give in direct proportion to a person's willingness to give. "Give, and it shall be given unto you; good measure, pressed down, and shaken together, and running over. . . .For with the same measure that ye mete withal it shall be measured to you again" (Luke 6:38). (See also II Corinthians 9:6-7.) It is not to be thought that a church can buy revival with giving, but by giving in accordance with God's plan the members can align themselves with God and be receptive to revival.

The final three steps not only foster revival, but maintain it within the church:

*Witnessing.* When Christians busy themselves in the matter of sharing the gospel of Jesus Christ, revival will continue. Sharing one's testimony with the lost not only benefits those with whom the gospel is shared but it also helps to maintain that person's experience with God. An active program of evangelism in a congregation of believers will create excitement and a spirit of revival. As members witness to lost souls, they see others come to Christ which keeps a flame of renewal and revival burning in their own souls. The entire church then matures and is benefited by it.

*Busy people.* Involved, busy Christians are happy Christians. They do not have time to gossip and spread rumors concerning others. They are totally immersed in the purpose of the church—reaching the world with true Bible salvation.

The old saying has merit, "If you want to get a job done, ask someone to do it who is busy." Often, people who are not busy are that way by choice. They probably have things they could do but simply are not motivated. Those who are busy usually want to be busy. Perhaps they have learned that one of the keys to a healthy, spiritual relationship with God is staying involved in His work.

There is a job for every person in God's kingdom and a person for every job. As a Christian involves himself in the kingdom of God, he will find himself happy about life, renewed daily in the Holy Spirit. If an idle mind is the devil's workshop, then a busy mind must be the hub of activity in Christian involvement.

*Worship.* Finally, a church must maintain a continual program of true worship of God. God still seeks men who will worship Him in Spirit and in truth (John 4:23-24). Worship feeds revival. The more a church worships, the better prepared their hearts will be to receive total spiritual renewal.

True worship is alive and it spreads that spiritual life to all who contact it. A church can worship its way through every trial, problem and battle. Revival will come to those who know how to worship God as true worshipers.

As a church follows these steps along the way of revival, renewal will come. Spiritual renewal on a daily basis is the key to obtaining spiritual healing and experiencing growth and maturity within the body of Christ. "Not by works of righteousness which we have done, but according to his mercy he saved us, by the washing of regeneration, and renewing of the Holy Ghost" (Titus 3:5).

Is there healing balm for the church today? Yes, and an ample supply for those who are willing to seek a diagnosis, receive the prescriptions of God's Word, and "take the medicine." The Great Physician is alive and well and ready to minister to every need of His growing church.

**Test Your Knowledge**

True or False

_____ 1. A church needs revival when divisions exist among the members.

_____ 2. When Christians become carnal, they lose sight of spiritual goals and become critical and sensitive.

_____ 3. Carnal people would rather pray about the faults of fellow Christians than gossip.

_____ 4. There is nothing wrong with a church just because souls are not being born again.

_____ 5. Apathy and unconcern are symptoms of spiritual disease.

_____ 6. Financial giving to God's work is a holy and natural activity for a Christian.

_____ 7. Jesus Christ's atoning death on Calvary purchased only our natural healing from sickness.
_____ 8. Revival is the general prescription which will bring spiritual health to any congregation.
_____ 9. Revival does not necessarily cause Christian growth and maturity in a child of God.
_____ 10. Old-fashioned prayer and fasting are only two of the many steps toward revival and spiritual healing.

## Apply Your Knowledge

People are the vessels God uses to cause revival in His church. Every major revival through history can be pinpointed to beginning with only one or a few persons. Frank Ewart, C. P. Kilgore, A. D. Urshan, O. F. Fauss, and others have started significant revivals because of an intense burden to see the church prosper.

*You* can be the key to revival—in your church, city, state, nation or even world. Purpose in your heart to hunger after revival for God's church and be willing to allow it to start with yourself. Work in conjunction with your pastor to see organized prayer and fasting, witnessing and soulwinning campaigns, worship at church and home and a renewal of faithfulness in attendance and giving to God's work.

## Expand Your Knowledge

When a church is revived spiritually, it is only then capable of being the ministering body of Christ. This is the subject of chapter eleven. Read each verse of Scripture in preparation for study of the chapter.

Try to do something especially good for someone this week. You will not only bless others, but yourself as well by being the ministering person God designed you to be.

# The Ministering Church

*For to their power, I bear record, yea, and beyond their power they were willing of themselves; Praying us with much intreaty that we would receive the gift, and take upon us the fellowship of the ministering to the saints. And this they did, not as we hoped, but first gave their own selves to the Lord, and unto us by the will of God.*

*II Corinthians 8:3-5*

---

### Start With the Scriptures

Romans 15:25  
I Corinthians 16:15  
Ephesians 5:21-32  

Philippians 1:6-11  
I Thessalonians 3:1-10

---

When one pauses to observe the life of Jesus Christ, he immediately notices the many wonderful attributes portrayed. From all vantage points, even the casual observer finds much to be admired. His character was beyond reproach. His deeds were not soiled or stained by the least trace of selfishness. The multitudes crowded around Jesus just to be near Him. The winding streets were packed with happy followers. The cities resounded with glad shouts and rejoicing.

What drew the multitudes to Christ? No doubt there are countless and varied reasons why they followed Him. Although probably no two reasons were exactly the same, there was possibly a common denominator among all the reasons. Perhaps many different problems had initially motivated them to seek help, but many ultimately journeyed long miles to personally present their own requests to the Christ because it was rumored that He was One who could meet needs!

In the Old Testament, Jehovah God revealed Himself to Moses as the "I Am." What He was actually saying was, "You go and do My will, and I will accompany you and be whatever you need Me to be. When you need provision, 'I Am' Jehovah-jireh, your provider. When you need peace, 'I Am' Jehovah-shalom, your peace. When you need healing, 'I Am' Jehovah-rapha, your healer." In short, the Lord said to Israel that He was their God, and regardless of their need, if they would trust Him, He would minister to them and meet it.

When God manifested Himself in flesh and came to the world as a man, He did not change. He was still the God who loved to minister to and meet the needs of the people who would believe in Him. When this news was broadcast, the needy of the nations searched until they found Him. While Jesus was despised by the religious hierarchy of His day, He was much loved and affectionately desired by those with troubles. They crowded Him out of the cities and into the open places where He could minister to them all. He met needs!

To the demoniac of Gadara, Jesus was the powerful deliverer from demon possession and the restorer of a right mind. To the widow at Nain, He was the brilliant resurrectionist and the bringer of joy. He gave her life back to her when He called her son back from the world beyond. To the embarrassed at a wedding celebration, He was the compassionate Creator who made water into wine just to spare them humiliation at an important hour. To the seeker of truth, He was the teacher who simplified the wisdom of the ages and presented it through choice illustrations. It was as though everywhere He went there was a sign hung out, "NEEDS MET HERE!" All with needs came and became a part of what was going on. Jesus met needs and people followed Him.

## Ministry to Needs

The key to Jesus' popularity with the people was that He ministered to them in a way that met their needs. Why do people go to a well? Because it is pretty, or because it meets their need? Why do folks draw close together and encircle a fire on a cold night? It is because doing so meets their need as they all seek warmth. Why do young men and women pay precious dollars to attend a college where they must slave to make grades high enough to remain? Because it is required by law, or because the education they receive promises to meet their future needs? It is need that motivates all of these as they seek to have those needs met.

The Apostle Paul was not an imposing figure to behold, and he stated that he did not come with the enticing words of man's wisdom; yet he was perhaps the most effective evangelist that has ever lived. Why? It is because everywhere he ministered he met needs. He was full of the Holy Ghost, and his ministry was through the demonstration of God's power. At times he convicted; at other times he comforted. He often challenged and, afterwards, encouraged. He always discerned the needs in the lives of those to whom he ministered and then found a way to meet them.

More than anything else, the church today needs to function in the same way as Christ and His chief apostles in the Early Church. People should think of the church in the same way they think of a well—"If I can just get to the house of God, I know my thirst will be quenched." The church should minister after the order of Paul—not in the enticing words of man's wisdom, but in the demonstration of the power of God! People need to know that if they are thirsty and desiring a refreshing, their needs can be met if they can only come in contact with Christ's church.

## Ministering Members of the Body

Churches that are unhappy do not grow, but it seems that happy churches always grow. A person can safely conclude that for a church to really grow, its people must be very happy.

What makes people happy? What is the common denominator among those who share an abundance of joy? Happy churches are full of people who are happy because they are being ministered to and their needs are being met.

The next logical question is, how are the happy people who make up the body of believers in these growing churches having their needs met? Their needs are being met through the concerned ministry of all the other members of the body. They are happy and strong because when they have a need, some mature, sensitive brother or sister is close enough and caring enough to discern it, and after becoming aware of it, finds a way to meet it. The church whose members' needs are met is one where the saints have been perfected to do the work of the ministry and help one another.

The work of the pastor is not to single-handedly meet the needs of everyone in his congregation. If he is expected to do that or thinks that he must do that, the congregation he pastors will never be known as a place where needs are met. He will never be able to hang out a sign, "NEEDS MET HERE," for he cannot physically, emotionally or spiritually fill the bill.

The pastor does not have to directly meet the daily needs of each person in his congregation. However, what he must do, through his prayer, his teaching, and his example, is to develop maturity in the Christians he pastors, enabling them to do "the work of the ministry." (See Ephesians 4:11-16.) This work of the ministry Paul referred to is simply the discerning of others' needs and the compassionate ministering to them. This is the choice privilege offered to every child of God—the chance to minister directly to the need of another member of the body, causing the whole church to be strong.

A Christian should never go to church without recognizing a personal need and possessing a desire to see that need met in that service. He must determine that through faith he will be ministered to. If he comes to God's house without a known need, he may leave the house of God disappointed and empty-handed.

At the same time, a Christian should never go to God's house without a plan to minister to someone else. "Oh, God, I come to Your house with a need. I know that You will use someone to minister to me. But, Lord, while You minister to me, I'm going to minister to someone else, in worship, in prayer, in fellowship, with a smile, through a kind word, by sharing a warm embrace. Oh, Lord, help me to be sensitive to Your leading in this service to feel the need in Your body and minister to it for you."

The best way for a Christian to stay spiritually healthy is by ministering to the other members of the body when they are weak and nursing them back to strength so they will be able to lift him up when he may be about to fall. If one fails to be sensitive to others and minister to their needs, there may come a time when there will be no one strong enough to meet his needs.

Christians need to hear the cries of the bleeding souls that come through the church doors. If only each one could be sensitive to God and discover the true needs of every visitor and fellow Christian alike who should be ministered to in that meeting. What would happen if every child of God would apply himself to being the Lord's hand extended to touch them?

All members of Christ's body compose the ministering church, and if they have the Holy Ghost, they have everything necessary to meet any spiritual need. The One known as the Comforter, Healer, Encourager, Convicter, Admonisher, Teacher, Lover, Patient Friend, Provider, Deliverer, Joy Bringer, and Perfect Peace dwells in the church members. God dwells in His people and through Him the needs of one another can be met.

The greatest commandment upon which all the other laws hang states that a man must love the Lord his God with all his heart, soul and mind (Matthew 22:35-40). Furthermore, the second commandment, which is joined to the first, states that a man must also love his neighbors as himself.

How does one go about loving the Lord like this? How does he love his neighbors as himself? It is being concerned enough about their happiness to be alert to their needs and then finding ways to minister to those needs.

Christ comforted His disciples just shortly before He was to be taken from them. They were all frightened at the prospect of His departure, and He proceeded to encourage them with these words, "A new commandment I give unto you, That ye love one another; as I have loved you, that ye also love one another. By this shall all men know that ye are my disciples, if ye have love one to another" (John 13:34-35). In other words, He was telling them that up until this time He had loved them by being attentive to their needs of all kinds and ministering to them. Now He said, "I must leave you, but there is no cause for alarm. What I have done in loving you, you will now perform for one another." Of course, He knew that in a few days He would return in the Spirit to dwell in them and, as such, He would help them to discern and meet one another's needs in the same way He had previously done.

Every Christian is part of the ministering church. The Spirit of God in us now allows us to do for one another what He would personally do for us if He were standing in flesh in our midst. The ministering church is not a building, nor is it a program or series of programs. The ministering church is that body of mature believers, full of the Holy Ghost and led of the Spirit, that discovers the areas of need in one another's lives and devises ways to minister to those needs.

Jesus once related a story which revealed that those who made it into Heaven made it as a result of their ministry to others (Matthew 25:31-46). They showed their love for Christ by loving His children enough to be sensitive to their needs and taking steps to meet them. Jesus said, "As you helped the least of these, you were ministering unto Me." The ones who missed Heaven missed it because they did not love enough to sense the problems in the lives of their brethren, God's children, and failed to help them. The Lord told these insensitive and unconcerned souls that in failing to assist their brothers, they had failed to minister unto Him and His needs went unprovided for.

Oh, what a privilege to be able to see a need in

another's life and be strong enough and wise enough to know how to meet it, for in so doing, we are able to minister unto God! Oh, that every Christian would submit himself unto his pastor as unto the Lord that he might be perfected for the ministry of noticing problems in his brothers and ministering strength unto them!

All Christians compose the ministering church. Every person who walks through the church doors has a need. It is God's plan that someone in the church body recognize and meet that need. All Christians should be willing to be that someone.

God's plan is that every believer be a functioning member of the church body. He then intends for these believers to look out for, care about, minister to, and build up one another.

Apostle Paul talked about this plan in detail in his letter to the Ephesians. He encouraged them to "speak the truth in love." As they did, they were told that they may "grow up into him in all things, which is the head, even Christ: From whom the whole body fitly joined together and compacted by that which every joint supplieth. . .maketh increase of the body unto the edifying of itself in love" (Ephesians 4:15-16).

## Twelve Ministries to One Another

The New Testament writers often encouraged the believers to do those things that would strengthen the other members of the body that they all might grow spiritually. Often the word used to describe this beautiful, natural and reciprocal process was translated "one another." In fact, not counting the Gospels, the word was used fifty-eight times in the New Testament.

Many of these admonitions are repeated from letter to letter, but when all the "one another" exhortations are carefully studied and grouped together, they can be reduced to perhaps twelve significant ministries Christians are to employ to meet the needs of and build up the body of Christ.

First, the church is admonished to minister love to one another. Out of this the other ministries grow. The other eleven ministries are:
- Know that we are members of one another (Romans 12:5)
- Be kindly affectioned (devoted love) to one another (Romans 12:10)
- Honor one another (Romans 12:10)
- Be of the same mind with one another (Romans 15:5)
- Accept one another (Romans 15:7)
- Admonish one another (Romans 15:14)
- Greet one another (Romans 16:3-6, 16)
- Serve one another (Galatians 5:13)
- Bear one another's burdens (Galatians 6:2)
- Bearing with one another (Ephesians 4:2)
- Submit to one another (Ephesians 5:21)

Yes, the church that grows is a happy church, and the reason it is happy is that all the members of that church family have most of their present needs met and know that their remaining problems are right now in the process of being solved.

Their needs are not all being met because they have a super pastor who mothers all of them through all types of trials, both small and great, each day. Their needs are met because they have a pastor who has opened their eyes to the fact that they do not just attend a ministering church, but they are the ministering church, and the church will ultimately be only as strong as its individual members.

They rejoice in the knowledge that they have the exciting privilege of strengthening the church through their own personal ministry to others. Their needs are met because each benefits from the joint ministry of every other sensitive, concerned, aware, wanting-to-help member of the body. What Jesus personally did in meeting the needs of the disciples, He now does through His children as He directs their ministries to one another.

You would probably say that you have faith in God and that is a wonderful thing, but did you know that there is even something more wonderful than that? There is! You can live your life in such a way that God begins to develop real faith and confidence in you. It is important that God have faith in us for it is the faith God has in us rather than the amount of faith we have in Him that determines the level of ministry He calls us to in His body.

When God shows you a need in the body, respond immediately. Don't hesitate! If you hesitate, the Lord may feel that you are not interested in ministering to others and He may cease showing you these opportunities for service. However, the more you respond to the needs of others, the greater is the confidence of God in your ministry in the church and the greater will be your level of service.

Ministering to others and strengthening the Lord's body is the greatest privilege in the world. In fact, it's what our salvation is all about! You are the ministering church.

### Test Your Knowledge

1. Multitudes followed Christ because He could meet their _____.

2. God even revealed Himself to Moses in the Old Testament as the "_____."

3. People need to feel confident that their needs will be met at _____.

4. A _____ should never go to church without the desire to have his needs met and meet the needs of others.

5. A Christian can stay spiritually _____ by ministering to the needs of other members of the body.

6. To effectively minister to the needs of others, we must be _____ to the Spirit.

7. By Christians' _____ for each other, they are recognized as Christ's disciples.

8. Every Christian is part of the ministering church when the _____ dwells within him.

9. The church is to bear one another's _____.

10. The church that _____ is a happy church, and it is happy because its _____ are being supplied through Christ.

## Apply Your Knowledge

Create a "burden book." This is a small book that you can carry with you to church. When needs are mentioned, make notes that you may later pray about those needs. If a brother or sister seems to be depressed, write down his or her name. Hold that individual up before God in prayer, and send a special card or do something special. Thoughtfulness and sensitivity to the Spirit for the needs of others are precious commodities.

## Expand Your Knowledge

The next chapter is a very practical one on taking advantage of the time we have. Read the foundation Scriptures before studying the chapter. If possible, obtain a copy of *How to Manage Your Time and Your Life* by Alan Lakein. You will find it most helpful on this subject.

# Redeeming the Time

*Redeeming the time, because the days are evil.*

*Ephesians 5:16*

---

### Start With the Scriptures

Proverbs 6:6
Ecclesiastes 3:1-17
Mark 13:33
Luke 19:44

I Corinthians 4:5
Ephesians 1:10
Hebrews 5:12
Revelation 1:3

---

### Time is Wealth

"Redeeming the time"—time is a valuable commodity, use it wisely, don't waste it (Ephesians 5:16).

Some people complain that if they only had the same opportunities afforded others, they could have accomplished so much in life. They, too, could have been successful.

Others wish the world's wealth might be equally divided to every person. This would provide each one the same opportunity. But, in a short time, a few would again control the world's resources. Why?

Because not everyone has the same ability and some who have it do not use it.

While God may not have given everyone the same ability, He has given to each person exactly the same quantity of time. He has blessed each one with equal wealth in this area of life. No one can hoard time and save it for the future. No one can borrow time from another. Each has the same amount given to him every day. Paul said, "Live life, then, with a due sense of responsibility, not as men who do not know the meaning and purpose of life but as those who do. Make the best use of your time, despite all the difficulties of these days" (Ephesians 5:15-16, *Phillips*).

## Planning Ahead

Israel's wise men believed in planning ahead. Solomon challenged the "sluggard" to consider the ant. This tiny creature has no supervisor to direct him and he attends no seminars on motivation, yet he carefully plans for his future. "Go to the ant, thou sluggard; consider her ways, and be wise: Which having no guide, overseer, or ruler, Provideth her meat in the summer, and gathereth her food in the harvest" (Proverbs 6:6-8).

Jesus also taught us to "count the cost" when considering the commitment of discipleship. He reminded us that anyone who would contemplate building a tower must first sit down, determine its cost, and then decide whether or not he has sufficient resources to complete the project. Otherwise, he may discover too late that he has only a partially completed building and then suffer ridicule for his carelessness.

Busy people have many demands placed upon them—work, home, family, church, personal devotion. This is a world filled with demands. Some people are unable to meet these expectations and withdraw into an unreal world of fantasy where they do little but "dream" of accomplishment. Others seem to be able to manage their time effectively and produce valuable contributions for themselves and others.

In the beginning, God ordained that man should not only work but also reap the rewards of his labor. Attaining goals through planning and work can be highly rewarding. Some goals are more easily reached than others. Some require great personal sacrifice of time and energy but provide a strong sense of accomplishment and satisfaction.

God has a plan for every life, a plan He ordained before the world began! To be an integral part of such a magnificent plan is indeed awesome and exciting! "The eyes of your understanding being enlightened; that ye may know what is the hope of his calling, and what the riches of the glory of his inheritance in the saints" (Ephesians 1:18).

All of a person's planning should be centered in Christ and His will. There is so much about life and eternity a person does not know. Christians must do their best with the resources they have available and leave the results in His hands. Jesus said to "occupy till I come." When a person does everything in his power to carry out God's will, God reserves some wonderful surprises for him. At the most unexpected times, He will breathe upon what one has done and bless it and fit it into His magnificent plan.

## Setting Goals

Ari Kiev in his book, *Strategy for Daily Living,* stated: "Observing the lives of people who have mastered adversity, I have repeatedly noted that they have established goals and, irrespective of obstacles, sought with all their effort to achieve them." He continues by saying that these people possess the ability to concentrate all their energies on reaching difficult goals and will not be deterred until they have accomplished the feat, no matter how difficult.

For the Christian, simply setting goals is not enough. He must prayerfully consider Christ's will for his life. He does have a plan for everyone and He will direct his path. "Trust in the LORD with all thine heart; and lean not unto thine own understanding. In all thy ways acknowledge him, and he shall direct thy paths" (Proverbs 3:5-6).

Paul was sure that he could do "all things" through Christ who gave him the necessary strength (Philippians 4:13). Jesus said, "With God all things are possible" (Matthew 19:26). Some people don't set high goals for themselves because they don't believe they could ever reach them. The above promises assure Christians that they can, through Christ, achieve goals beyond their natural abilities. For this reason, a person must set his goals prayerfully. Once he has determined God's will, faith will give him the vision to reach the "impossible."

Have you ever thought about why you are here? Where do you want to go? Where does God want you to go? What does He want you to be? How can you become everything you are capable of being?

A person should take a few minutes to write down some goals he would like to achieve in his life. Some of these goals will be short term, others intermediate term, and some long term. For example, short-term goal might be something one would like to accomplish this next week. An intermediate goal could be something he would like to achieve next year.

Taking time to think about goals sets an important process in motion. He may not know just how he will get to where he wants to go but at least he has given some consideration to where he is headed.

Setting goals helps people feel good about themselves. There is nothing wrong with having positive feelings about ourselves. The Bible teaches that we are very important to Christ. He gave Himself for us. He died for us! He lives for us! He has prepared a place for us in His great plan. Even the angels would like to participate in the experience He has given to His children (I Peter 1:12).

Reaching goals that have already been set gives a person a sense of accomplishment. This encourages him to set further goals and to press toward them. People who don't set goals have no real sense of purpose in life. Hence they do not feel their lives are worthwhile.

## Watch Out for Sharks!

James warned that people who have no faith toss aimlessly on the sea of life and may be destroyed in a storm (James 1:5-7). Goals help us determine where we are going. Strategy helps us get there.

The fable of the sea horse is a case in point. The sea horse decided to seek his fortune. He gathered his money together and started out. Soon he met an eel who asked, "Hello, friend. Where are you going?"

"I'm going to seek my fortune," replied the sea horse proudly.

"This is your lucky day," proclaimed the eel. "For three silver pieces you may have this flipper to speed you on your way."

"How wonderful," replied the sea horse. He paid his money and was quickly on his way. Now he could travel twice as fast!

Soon he met a sponge who asked, "Where are you going in such a hurry?"

The sea horse replied, "Why, I'm going to seek my fortune."

"Here is a fine jet scooter that will take you five times as fast. It's yours for just ten pieces of silver."

"That's reasonable," thought the sea horse, and he was soon speeding over the waves faster than he had ever imagined possible.

A short time later he met a shark who asked, "Where are you going on that fine scooter?"

"To seek my fortune," replied the sea horse.

"Do you know how to get there?" queried the shark.

"Well, no, but I will surely get there quickly at this speed," the sea horse reassured.

"This is your lucky day," cried the shark. "If you will take this short cut," said the shark, pointing to his open mouth, "you will save yourself a lot of time."

"Thanks so much," replied the unsuspecting sea horse as he sped into the dark caverns of the shark's stomach!

Satan has goals for us too! It is vital that we prayerfully determine Christ's goals for our lives and then seek His help in achieving them.

## Types of Goals

Long-range goals are our most important goals. What will I accomplish with the life God has given me? This is a big question but the answer may not be apparent to us for a number of years. Other long-range goals may be easier to identify. However, it is easy for a person to become depressed just standing and looking at his long-range goals, wondering how he will ever get there.

First, long-range goals should be divided into intermediate goals. For example, a young person may feel God's call to be a missionary to a certain country. He may never get there unless he prepares himself. Intermediate goals might include formal education in language studies, Bible school, and/or other pertinent fields. Another intermediate goal would be gaining experience in some areas of ministry. Such a background will help achieve his primary goal.

Short-range goals are important because, without them, people cannot achieve the things that mean the most to them. As can be seen, one reaches his important goals by breaking down the tasks into simpler units he can reach in a short time.

In the above example, the young person would begin by deciding what school he wished to attend in order to study the required subjects to reach his intermediate-range goals. Once he has settled on the school, he must think about how he will pay for his education. When he finally arrives at the school, he is faced with the task of making decisions about his time. How much time will he devote to his studies, to work, devotion, church, and social life?

All of these competitive interests constantly vie for his attention, but unless he keeps his goal of completing his education clearly in mind, he may become distracted by other activities and not reach his desired goal.

What will he do when he completes his education? What opportunities should he consider in the ministry? How will he know when God has opened a door for him? How much experience will he need before he is ready to apply for a missionary appointment? The answers to these questions are complex, but he will find them as he works each day to achieve his long-range goals in the will of God. The Lord will also provide opportunities for him to talk with experienced men who will be able to give him guidance in making these decisions.

How can a person help a billion starving people or a million homeless? If he thinks about it, the task is awesome and far beyond his capabilities. At this point he may shrug his shoulders and tell himself, "It's just too much for one person." This is true, but one eleven-year-old boy decided he could do something about it. He started by helping one homeless person find shelter. Then he helped another. Even at his young age, he had discovered that short-range goals are essential in achieving the long-range goals of life.

The Apostle Paul explained that he did not dwell on the failures of his past. Rather, he kept his eyes fixed on the goal of winning the prize, the high calling he had in Christ Jesus (Philippians 3:13-14).

How did Paul achieve that long-range goal? He lived day by day, walking in Christ. As he faced death, he could say with confidence, "I have fought a good fight, I have finished my course, I have kept the faith: Henceforth there is laid up for me a crown of righteousness, which the Lord, the righteous judge, shall give me at that day: and not to me only, but unto all them also that love his appearing (II Timothy 4:7-8).

## What Is Most Important?

The importance of establishing long-range goals and achieving them by setting intermediate and short-range goals, taking one step at a time has been discussed. But how does a person decide upon which goals to focus? There are many worthwhile goals one might have for his life, but he may not be able to achieve them all. In fact, he could soon become confused and be unable to act effectively if he tried to work toward all of them simultaneously.

Do we really know what is most important for our lives? How can we know when we understand so little about God's plan for us as it fits into His great master plan? Some people have been unable to feel any definite direction for their lives. Consequently, they don't do anything.

Jesus taught that Christians should do something. They may not grasp all He has planned for their future, but they can set some realistic goals and achieve them. The man whom Jesus condemned in the parable of the "talents" was the man who did nothing because he was afraid he would fail (Matthew 25:14-30). Jesus said the servant could have at least taken the money to the bank and invested it. Just about anyone can do that.

As a Christian matures, he may change his priorities. Sometimes young people look at certain positions of leadership as the goals they want to achieve. Years later, after having achieved such a goal, they may re-evaluate their priorities and feel the Lord is leading them in a new direction.

Life is learning, re-evaluating, and moving forward. Forward to what? To the ultimate purpose Christ has for us. Granted, we make a number of mistakes along the way, but we have no fear of falling by the wayside when we place our lives in His capable hands.

He will help us with our mistakes, guide us over the rough spots, forgive us for our selfishness when we insist on having our own way. Truly, we can do all things through Christ who gives us strength and direction (Philippians 4:13).

## Facing Obstacles

The inability to achieve a much desired goal can be most frustrating and disappointing. It can discourage a person from setting new goals. After all, if he cannot achieve one goal, why should he try anything else?

All Christians have different personalities—different ways of reacting to situations. While some people may be dismayed over their inability to achieve an important goal, others see it as a challenge to seek an alternative strategy and attack the problem with zest.

Some people who experience such frustration wish they were more like the others who forge ahead. But wishing to be like someone else will not solve the problem at hand. What can be done now about the present problem? Is this goal realistic? Have we reached too high for this time in our lives?

Realistic goals can be reached and people feel good about themselves when they get there. The pastor of a church of one hundred people is probably setting an unrealistic goal if he announces, "Let's shoot for five hundred in attendance next Sunday!" The people know that unless he has a "rabbit in his hat," they will not have five hundred next Sunday. So why even try? However, if he had set the goal at 125 and offered some suggestions as to how it could be reached, he might generate enthusiasm. Next week, when the members saw an increase, they would be motivated to continue trying.

Setting unrealistic goals is not a person's only source of frustration. Another problem may be an unforeseen barrier that prevents him from reaching a goal he perceived as quite realistic. It may not be possible for him to remove the barrier, to climb over it, or to go around it. He has been stopped cold! What now?

What is the cause of the barrier? Is it psychological, social, economic, physical, or spiritual? It helps to identify the cause. If it is not identified, valuable time is wasted misdirecting energies toward false causes. It is easy to blame the devil for all of our problems. Satan does go about "as a roaring lion. . .seeking whom he may devour" (I Peter 5:8). However, the barrier one faces may be something over which he has little control. It is also possible that the Lord has placed a barrier before him.

We cannot go wrong when we trust the Lord with our lives and prayerfully make our decisions. We will make mistakes, possibly many of them, but He knows how to bring victory out of failure. If Satan is frustrating a goal Christ wills us to achieve, the Lord will help us overcome the enemy's power.

Possibly the Lord wants to teach us some valuable lessons in patience and in the art of complete trust. The goal may be in His will, but He may wish to guide us there through an alternate route in order to teach us something we need to know that we had not considered. Some people are impatient. They want "all or nothing!" They may balk at the thought of accepting something less than the goal they were determined to achieve, but that may be His will.

Prayer changes things and changes people— changes their attitudes, their outlook, their view of God, others, and of themselves. As Paul declared, we can do anything as long as we walk with Christ and believe Him for the "impossible."

We do not have to waste the valuable resource of time God has given to each of us. By establishing priorities, setting realistic goals, and trusting Him, we can indeed "redeem the time."

## Test Your Knowledge

1. Everyone has the same quantity of _____.
2. Israel's wise men believed in _____.
3. Jesus taught us to _____ the cost when considering the commitment of discipleship.
4. There are many _____ placed upon our time.
5. For the Christian, his _____ should be based upon the will of God for his life.
6. There are short-term, intermediate, and

_____ goals.

7. _____ goals are the most important goals in one's life.

8. As we mature, we may change our _____.

9. Setting unrealistic goals causes _____.

10. Realistic goals can be _____, and it causes us to feel good about ourselves.

## Apply Your Knowledge

Why not have a goal planning and goal setting session? Where would you like to be five years from now, and what do you want to be doing? You can only hit the targets in life for which you aim.

The first step is to evaluate where you are presently and to determine a realistic, but challenging, goal for five years from now. When you have established these long-range goals, the next step is to determine intermediate and short-range goals which will guide you toward your long-range goals.

The short-range goals can be regularly examined and adjusted to help you meet the intermediate goals, and the intermediate goals will then take you on to the long-range goals.

You should also continue to expand your long-range goals, always maintaining some goals at least five years distant. Remember to always prayerfully include the Holy Spirit in your planning that He may direct your paths in His will.

## Expand Your Knowledge

Prepare for chapter thirteen by reading all the Scriptures at the beginning of the chapter. They will prepare you for this vital and final chapter on the importance of submission. You will observe how submission to authority made Moses a great man of God.

# My Place in My World

*Submitting yourselves one to another in the fear of God.*

*Ephesians 5:21*

---

### Start With the Scriptures

Ezekiel 33:1-11; 34:1-10  
Matthew 20:25-28  
Acts 20:28-38  
Romans 13:1-7  
Ephesians 5:21-33  
I Thessalonians 2:1-13  
Hebrews 13

---

Who would believe his report? How could he ever adequately describe such a marvelous experience with God? Moses had been minding his own business tending sheep on the side of Mount Sinai when his attention was drawn to a large bush that was aflame but not consumed.

Hurrying over to the fire, Moses was startled by an audible voice which spoke from the bush and told him to take off his shoes because he was on holy ground! Who would believe the account of such an event? Why, Moses himself could hardly believe what God was saying. But the message was clear and there was no room for confusion.

Moses had been seeking direction for his life since he had fled Egypt to escape a murder charge. This encounter with God was his answer! Now that he had personal direction, how should he respond? How would this affect his present relationships?

He was employed, he reminded himself. Jethro was his father-in-law in addition to being his employer. That could complicate matters! Would his wife, Zipporah, understand what God was doing in her husband's life? Would she accept it as the will of God and cooperate? Obedience to God would involve many changes for everyone concerned.

## Respect for Others

Some people who have had a marvelous experience with God have responded as if they did not care what other people thought. In their exhilaration following their divine experience, they felt so superior to parents, spouse, pastor, or employer that they did not bother to acquire their input and counsel. After all, if they had just spoken with God, that was all they needed. Or so they thought.

Moses certainly cherished his moment alone with the Lord. Those moments had healed his wounded self-esteem from a foiled attempt to help Israel in their captivity. The voice of the Lord had quieted the calliope within him and had given direction to his nomadic thoughts.

Not only was Moses in fellowship with God, but he was also joined together with other people. No man is an island. He affects and is affected by others. No one lives or dies without affecting others to some degree. (See Romans 14:7.) It cannot be avoided. If Moses was going to carry out this God-ordained mission, he would need the cooperation and goodwill of many people.

God called Moses while he was submitted to Jethro, a Midianite priest. For this reason Moses felt it was imperative that he consult with his father-in-law. Despite the fact he probably had obtained a deeper experience with God than anyone of his immediate acquaintance, Moses still sensed his need of Jethro! If God was able to speak to Moses, He was also capable of dealing with Jethro about this mission.

## Strength Through Submission

Moses had an outstanding ministry with enduring results because he had learned two important principles.

*First, he accepted the fact that he had a unique calling of God on his life.* He would not spend fruitless moments comparing himself with others because God had asked him to accomplish a specific task.

*Secondly, he accepted the fact that no matter how powerful his ministry, there would always be people over and under him in authority.* Even as Moses was leading Israel toward Canaan and exercising tremendous authority, he submitted to the advice of his father-in-law. (See Exodus 18.)

T. F. Tenney has said that if the Bible could be reduced to one word, it would be the word *submission*. The Apostle Paul wrote to the Ephesians, "Submitting yourselves one to another in the fear of God" (Ephesians 5:21).

While much attention is often given to his "burning bush" experience with God, some of Moses' greatest character traits were exhibited in his response to God's call. Even in his response to the call of God, Moses continued to respect those in authority over him. "And Moses went and returned to Jethro his father in law, and said unto him, Let me go, I pray thee, and return unto my brethren which are in Egypt, and see whether they be yet alive. And Jethro said to Moses, Go in peace" (Exodus 4:18).

## Accountability

A Benjamite of the New Testament who also had an extraordinary experience with God responded in a similar fashion. In his personal testimony, the Apostle Paul indicated that he felt the need of accountability. "And I went up by revelation, and communicated unto them that gospel which I preach among the Gentiles, but privately to them which were of reputation, lest by any means I should run, or had run, in vain" (Galatians 2:2).

Not only was Moses responsible to Jethro, but in his excitement he was not to forget his duties to his immediate family. On the family's journey to Egypt to carry out the will of God, the Lord apparently sought to kill Moses by making him severely ill (Exodus 4:24-25). Moses had failed as a father to perform the ancient covenant token of circumcision on his own son. If he was going to lead God's people, he could not ignore the commandments given to those people. The leader's son could not be a part of Israel if he was not circumcised. Zipporah performed the circumcision rite, probably because her husband was too sick to do so. When everything was in divine order in his family, Moses was healed and able to continue his journey.

## Finding Our Place in God's Plan

One of the innate drives within every person is the need to be authentic. Something deep within the human soul craves purposeful living—a meaningful place of service where individual gifts and abilities can be used to the fullest extent.

Everyone wants his life to be meaningful to others and would want to be missed if he were not fulfilling his place in life. All Christians should realize that they may not excel at everything in life, but all would probably like to do something well and be a craftsman in some area of life.

God has established rhyme, reason, and meticulous order in both the natural and spiritual realms. Every part of God's kingdom, no matter how insignificant it may appear, is very important to the successful function of the whole. It is extremely important for each Christian to discover and then be loyal to his calling. He must function in his God-given place and at the same time submit himself to the authority of those over him.

## Protection Through Submission

Submission to authority provides a unique protection for the individual under authority as well as the one in authority. Power, authority, and protection all flow together in a unique relationship designed by God in the structure of authority.

Jesus once complimented a man, "I have not found so great faith, no, not in Israel" (Luke 7:9). This was His response to the observation of a Roman centurion. The officer had said that it would not be necessary for the Lord to come physically to his home to heal his servant. For one thing, the centurion felt unworthy of such an honored guest. But secondly, he had an insight about power. He told Jesus that He could just speak the work and healing would take place.

The soldier was referring to his experience of working under the military chain of command and authority. He knew as he patrolled the region around

Galilee that he was not acting alone. He was not there of his own will but was obeying the instructions of those who were over him. His authority came from Caesar, and when he spoke, it was as if the emperor himself had uttered the words. Those who served under the centurion must submit and obey him, or they were answerable to Caesar from whom the officer had received his orders. By submitting to those over him, the centurion was protected to function with power in his place.

This officer, working within the military chain of command, understood more about Jesus' ministry than even His disciples who had spent so much time with the Lord. The Roman knew that Jesus was not just a man acting alone. He was there to do the pleasure and will of the One who sent Him. All creation must obey Him in the same way that soldiers and peasants followed the orders of the centurion.

The Apostle Paul reminded the Corinthian church of the chain of authority God had established from the beginning (I Corinthians 11:3). Children were under their parents; the women were under the men; and the men were under Christ. God established this order of authority as a matter of protection and benefit to His creation. He knew that the weaknesses of human flesh could be strengthened by a sound plan of submission to authority. Happiness is achieved by submitting to this inevitable law of the creation.

In order for the church, the family, and individuals to be happy and properly protected, everyone must find and remain in his place. All sin, sickness, and problems from the time of Eve's transgression, can be traced back to the fact that she and Adam did not stay under the protective authority God provided.

What a different world people would be living in today had Eve sent the tempter to her head, Adam, who would have referred Lucifer to the God over him! When people step out from under authority, they leave themselves unprotected from temptation.

## Rebellion Brings Judgment

Any attempt by men to rearrange God's order or to circumvent His government is called "rebellion." When a person tries to change what God has established, he is really suggesting that the creature has a better plan than the Creator. This always leads to confusion and divine judgment.

Much emphasis in the study of the sixth chapter of Isaiah has been placed on the prophet's experience in the Temple. While not to overlook this holy audience with God, one should observe a previous condition that precipitated this spiritual crisis. A clue is found in the opening phrase of the chapter: "In the year that King Uzziah died I saw also the Lord sitting upon a throne, high and lifted up, and his train filled the temple" (Isaiah 6:1).

King Uzziah was the national leader for fifty-two years. He had begun his reign when he was sixteen years old, and overall, he had been a good king and military genius. But toward the end of his reign something happened that brought drastic changes to the kingdom. "But when he was strong, his heart was lifted up to his destruction: for he transgressed against the LORD his God, and went into the temple of the LORD to burn incense upon the altar of incense" (II Chronicles 26:16).

The king knew better than to take such authority that was not his. He knew he was out of his place. Burning incense in the Temple was the function of the priestly office—not the king. When Azariah the high priest and eighty of the ministering priests discovered the king in the holy place, they attempted to stop him.

Uzziah became angry that these priests would have the audacity to tell him what he could and could not do. After all, he was the chief of state! He threatened to strike the priests with the consecrated censor. As he attempted to do so, God suddenly struck him with the dreadful disease of leprosy. There was immediate evidence of this very contagious disease, and the priests quickly ushered him out of the Temple.

King Uzziah was quarantined in a separate house away from the palace to keep others from contamination. His son, Jotham, served as a surrogate while Uzziah died the slow, painful death of a leper. He symbolizes all good men who get out of their proper place.

No one, no matter how good his record, can violate God's order of authority without suffering the consequences. God could not allow Uzziah to usurp unrightful authority in functioning as a priest. If God allowed Uzziah to subvert the authority of the priesthood, others would try it. The people would have lost respect for God's order of authority, and chaos would have resulted.

There is a certain judgment that falls upon people who are not content with God's order. Ironically, those who try to usurp authority lose even that authority which they did originally possess. A father loses the respect of his own family; a mother becomes frustrated with the rebellion of her children; a king loses his kingship. Uzziah lost the throne to which he was called because he tried to become a priest, which was out of the will of God.

Korah and his followers lost their place of honor as well as their lives when they rebelled against Moses. Miriam, Moses' sister, would have died with leprosy like Uzziah if Moses had not interceded before the Lord.

While King Uzziah remained alive in quarantine,

the nation continued under a cloud of confusion. Certainly Jotham was on the throne, but who was really in charge? Perhaps the people did not know if Uzziah was giving orders for his son to carry out or if Jotham was truly in command. Everything remained in limbo until Uzziah died.

## Revival of Divine Order

When the king finally succumbed to leprosy, the spirit of rebellion he represented died also. The confusion of order died. The uncertainty left and order was restored. The people then had a clear understanding of God's chain of command.

It was at this time that Isaiah went into the Temple—the very place where his leader had failed. It was from the Temple that the confusion of authority had arisen, and the restoration of order began at the Temple. The prophet saw the manifested glory of God as never before. The entire Temple reverberated with God's presence as angels, seraphims, and cherubims ministered to Isaiah.

The glory of God came into the Temple when divine order was restored. God's work does not progress well while people are in rebellion, out of fellowship with one another, and competing against each other. Rebellious members do not produce a coordinated effort of the body of believers. Fear and confusion develops and hinders the body of Christ.

In the glow of God's glory, Isaiah saw the true condition of himself as well as that of the people. In that holy atmosphere, Isaiah received clear direction for himself as well as for God's people. He understood where he fit into God's plan. By accepting God's order of authority, the royal prophet actually found a powerful and authentic ministry. It was lying under the mantle of submission.

Revival always comes to people who are joined in

love. Their unity is based on their mutual submission. Two major keys to revival are humility and unity. They can never be circumvented or ignored if revival is going to happen.

May God give the church the ability to learn from these examples of history. Failure to submit to authority has caused some men in past history to fall, but the church will not be deceived by that trap. As the church body continues to submit one member to another, and each member keeps his proper place, God's presence continues to be the vibrant force moving the church to total victory.

## Test Your Knowledge

### True or False

\_\_\_\_\_ 1. Moses would have been able to accomplish his task of leading Israel even without the help and cooperation of other people.

\_\_\_\_\_ 2. Moses maintained a submissive spirit toward his father-in-law, Jethro, despite his deeper experience with God.

\_\_\_\_\_ 3. Moses accepted his unique calling of God and yet recognized that there would always be someone in authority over him.

\_\_\_\_\_ 4. Moses' meekness was a weakness.

\_\_\_\_\_ 5. It is very important for every Christian to discover and be loyal to his calling.

\_\_\_\_\_ 6. Submission to authority provides a unique protection for the person under authority as well as the one in authority.

\_\_\_\_\_ 7. All sin and sickness can be traced back to Adam and Eve's departure from the pattern of authority.

_____ 8. When a person tries to change what God has established, he is only helping God.

_____ 9. God will judge all rebellion.

_____10. The unity within the church is based upon the mutual submission of every member.

## Apply Your Knowledge

Examine your relationships with others in the church to see if there might be room for improvement. List those with whom you feel you have less unity than God would desire. Think of possible ways to improve your relationship with them. Some possible suggestions are: working with them on various church projects; inviting them over for a meal and fellowship; going with them on an outing of some nature. There are many possibilities for developing that relationship.

Our goal as Christians should be to submit ourselves to one another in the fear of God. (See Ephesians 5:21.) As we endeavor to unify ourselves with other members of Christ's body, the church can experience greater revival.

## Expand Your Knowledge

There are many good books available to expand your horizons of thinking in the area of Christian service and maturity. One to be especially recommended is *Improving Your Serve* by Charles Swindoll. It is an excellent book for further maturity in the realm of Christian service. You may order it from the Pentecostal Publishing House, 8855 Dunn Road, Hazelwood, MO 63042-2299.

There are also other profitable studies in the **Word Aflame Elective Series.** You will want to collect each one.